SEASONS OF GRACE

52 DEVOTIONS FOR THE JOURNEY

CHARLES E. CRAVEY

IN HIS STEPS PUBLISHING

Scriptures are from the King James Version of the Holy Bible

ISBN: 978-1-58535-055-1 (Paper)

ISBN: 978-1-58535-056-8 (EPUB)

ISBN: 978-1-58535-010-0 (Hardback)

Library of Congress Catalog Number: 2025906035

Book and cover design by Charles E. Cravey and Book Brush.

Printed in the United States by:

IN HIS STEPS PUBLISHING, Statesboro, Georgia

CONTENTS

Dedication

To those seeking solace and strength in faith,

May these words illuminate your path,

Rekindle your spirit,

And guide you closer to the boundless love and grace of the Divine.

With gratitude for the countless blessings and unwavering inspiration that have shaped this journey, I humbly offer this work as a testament to faith and devotion.

From an early age, I've been writing poetry, articles, and sermons. God divinely gifted me with a passion for writing. This gift lets me share my thoughts, feelings, and life's reflections. I write to connect with others, inspiring and encouraging them with my words. Sharing my writing, which reflects God's grace and love, is a true privilege. My writing aims to comfort, inspire, and bring hope to my readers. I appreciate you letting me share God's blessings with you.

Start each of your Sundays with a chapter—it's perfect for family time or personal reflection. Listen to it and may God's spirit nourish you as it did me during the creation of these. May these poems enrich your devotion and reveal God's grace.

God bless each of you on this journey together.

The Rev. Dr. Charles E. Cravey, April 2025

Https://drcharlescravey.com

MY SOUL'S ETERNAL PEACE

"My Soul's Eternal Peace"

Charles E. Cravey

Adrift, I sailed the sea of strife.
Tossed by waves, the storms of life.
Lost in currents, no guiding hand,
No solid ground, just shifting sand.

But then, a force both firm and kind,
Reached through the chaos, eased my mind.
It pulled me close, gave strength anew,
Showed me the path I never knew.

Within my soul, I stand complete,
A steady heart, no fear to meet.
No drifting tides, no shadows bleak,
For in His love, I'M NEVER WEAK!

My eyes are fixed on God above,
He fills my heart with endless love.
Through every storm, His light does gleam,
A steadfast guide, my hope, my dream.

Now on the rock where hope stands strong,
I've found the place where I belong.
Salvation's light, a beacon grand,
My soul restored life's steady hand.

With grace, He lifts me, sets me free,
His love endures, eternally.

In this newfound peace, I find my way,
Embracing dawn with the Son's bright ray.
The world, once vast and filled with fear,
Now feels like home, with His presence near.

Every step I take is sure and bright,
Guided by faith and His gentle light.
No longer lost, no longer alone,
In His embrace, I've truly grown.

With courage renewed, I face each day,
Knowing His love will never sway.
A journey once fraught with endless night,
Transformed by grace into radiant light.

So here I stand, with joy profound,
My spirit uplifted, my heart unbound.
In the arms of love that never cease,
I've found my soul's eternal peace.

Scripture Reading: Psalm 23:4

"Yea, though I walk through the valley of the shadow of death, I will fear no evil: for thou art with me; thy rod and thy staff they comfort me." (Psalm 23:4)

Devotional: My Soul's Eternal Peace

How frequently do we meander through life, adrift and unmoored, lacking a compass or guiding light? Yet, even in the darkest moments, when the path seems obscured and the horizon distant, there is a glimmer of hope—a chance to find our bearings and steady our course. It is in these moments of uncertainty that we often discover the true depth of our resilience and the strength of our spirit.

As we navigate the winding roads of existence, we learn to seek the muted whispers of wisdom that guide us through the storms. We find solace in the gentle reminders of love and connection, which anchor us to a higher purpose and a sense of belonging.

This journey reminds us that every challenge is an opportunity for growth, and every setback teaches perseverance. With each step forward, we gather fragments of courage and shards of grace, piecing together a mosaic of hope and determination.

And so we continue onward, buoyed by an unwavering faith in the possibilities that lie ahead. For in the end, it is not the destination that defines us, but the journey and the love that accompanies us along the way. Embracing the unforeseen, we tread the path with open hearts, welcoming each experience as a teacher. Joy and sorrow weave the tapestry of life, yet within its intricate patterns, we find beauty and meaning. As we journey, we learn to cherish the moments of stillness, where reflection nurtures understanding and gratitude blooms.

In the quietude, we recognize the whispers of our own soul, urging us to listen, to feel, and to grow. We come to understand that true strength lies not in avoiding the storms but in facing them with courage and grace. Each challenge becomes a steppingstone, elevating us to new heights of wisdom and compassion.

And so, we walk this path together, hand in hand with those who share our journey. We draw strength from one another, our collective spirits forming a tapestry of love and unity. In the embrace of solidarity, we find the courage to dream, to hope, and to forge a future where kindness and understanding flourish.

Thus, we become the architects of our destiny, crafting a world illuminated by the light of our shared humanity. With hearts open wide, we step forward into the unknown, confident, knowing that love will always light our way.

As a young soul, I recall the trepidation that cloaked the night's shadows. I would frolic with my companions until twilight descended, then scamper homeward, leaping from one flickering streetlight to another, regaining my breath. With the passage of time, I now gaze back upon these moments and discern that the darkness held no peril; it was merely the shroud of obscurity that veiled my sight.

Wonder and curiosity took root within that obscurity. Each shadowy corner became a canvas for my imagination, painting stories of adventure and intrigue. The quiet rustle of leaves, the distant hoot of an owl, and the gentle hum of the night transformed into a symphony of possibilities, urging me to explore beyond the limits of my youthful fears.

As I grew, I realized that the darkness was not something to be feared but embraced, for it was within its depths that I discovered the light of understanding. Those twilight escapades taught me lessons that I wove into the fabric of my being, showing me how to see beyond the surface and trust the unseen forces that guide us.

Now, as I stand at the crossroads of life's journey, I carry with me the wisdom gleaned from those youthful nights. I recall that even when the path ahead is unclear, there is always an inner light—a spark of hope and courage—to guide me. It is this inner light that enables me to stride forward with confidence, embracing the unknown with a heart full of wonder and a spirit unafraid.

So, I continue to frolic through life, leaping from one moment of clarity to another, breathing in the surrounding beauty. For even in the shadows, there is grace, and in every step, a new adventure awaits, calling me to explore the vast tapestry of life with open eyes and an open heart.

Do not tremble in the shadows. The luminous presence of Christ forever illuminates our way, guiding and shaping our journey. With each step we take, His light casts away the darkness, revealing the path of love and purpose. In His warmth, the shadows of doubt and fear dissolve, leaving behind a trail of hope and renewal.

Every moment becomes an opportunity to grow in faith, as His eternal light encourages us to embrace the challenges before us with courage and trust. It is through this divine guidance that we find strength, not only for ourselves but also to uplift those around us.

Prayer:

Dear Lord, hear my plea in those dark days of my soul when I need replenishment and hope. Never let me stray too far from the fold. Guide my footsteps and keep me near thy Grace. With my heart, I pray to thee. Amen.

Reflection Questions:

1. If every moment is an opportunity to grow in faith, in what ways do you seek for that to happen?

2. What may you do today to be a beacon of light to those around you? In what ways could your life be light to others?

3. What may you do to enable your church to be more of a beacon to those outside the church?

2

Faithful Steps with the Lord

"Faithful Steps with the Lord"

Charles E. Cravey

Shape my footsteps, Lord, where they should go.

Never let them veer from the path You show.

Through valleys dim and mountains steep,

Be my guide, my soul to keep.

With each new day, Lord, may I be

Consecrated more to Thee.

Whenever I may drift or fall,

Be my anchor, strong and tall.

I will not fear the dread of night,

For You are there—my guiding light.

You are all my spirit needs.

I do not waver, Your faith decreed.

When shadows fall and doubts arise,

Lift my gaze to Your endless skies.

Grant me strength to face each day,

And faith to trust in Your perfect way.

When trials press and tempests roar,

I'll cling to You forevermore.

Your boundless grace, my heart sustains,

Through every joy and all my pain.

With mercy new at break of dawn,

I'll trust Your love to carry on.

For in Your hands, my life is whole,

Redeemed and sanctified in soul.

Scripture: Psalm 37:23

The steps of a good man are ordered by the Lord: and he delighteth in his way." —Psalm 37:23

Devotional: Faithful Steps with the Lord

As we journey through life, we often encounter uncertainties, trials, and moments when our path seems unclear. Yet, in these moments, God's guiding hand offers unwavering assurance. The poem "Faithful Steps with the Lord" is a heartfelt prayer of surrender and trust, a reminder that we are never alone on this walk of faith.

Each verse reflects the beauty of a life consecrated to God—seeking His direction, trusting His strength, and leaning on His unchanging grace. When we drift, He anchors us. When night falls and fears arise, He is our light. He doesn't promise a life without challenges, but He assures us of His presence, His sustenance, and His faithfulness every step of the way.

How often do we pause and invite God to shape our steps? This is not just a onetime decision but a daily commitment. With each new day, we have the chance to yield our plans, worries, and doubts to Him, trusting that His way is perfect and that His grace is sufficient.

Take heart, dear friend. Just as the psalmist wrote and the poem echoes, God orders the steps of those who trust in Him. No matter where you are today—whether on steady ground or facing a steep climb—know that the Lord is with you, guiding, anchoring, and lighting your path.

Prayer:

Lord, I surrender my steps to You today. Shape my path according to Your will and give me the faith to trust in Your perfect plan. Be my strength in times of weakness, my light in the darkness, and my anchor when the winds of life blow hard. I rest knowing that You are all my spirit needs. Amen.

Reflective Questions:

1. In what areas of your life do you need to surrender your plans to God's guidance?

2. How can you remind yourself daily of God's faithfulness and presence in your life?

3

THE MAESTRO'S GIFT

The Maestro's Gift

(In Honor of my dear friend, Dr. Jackson Borges)

Charles E. Cravey

Upon the keys, his fingers dance,

A symphony of soul, a sacred trance.

Each note ascends, a prayer takes flight,

Transforming hearts with heaven's light.

The organ sings, its voice divine.

A gift of grace. Through him, it shines.

Sunday morns, the church is still,

In raptured awe, all spirits fill.

His melodies, a whispered prayer,

Binding souls with love and care.

A maestro's touch, both pure and true,

A vessel of God's work to do.

Through music's flow, God's glory streams,

Awakening faith, restoring dreams.

For every heart his hymns impart,

The Maestro's gift—a sacred art.

Within each of us lies the potential to be a radiant blessing to those around us. My dear friend, Dr. Jackson Borges, embodies this truth through his divinely given talent as our church organist on Sundays. With exuberance and joy, he dances upon the keys, filling our cathedral with the uplifting melodies of praise that nourish our spirits each week.

What unique gift do you possess? Perhaps it's a talent for painting vivid scenes that captivate the imagination or a knack for storytelling that transports listeners to faraway worlds. Maybe it's a compassionate heart that offers comfort to those in need or an ability to make others laugh and lift their spirits. Each of us carries within a unique spark, a special ability that, when shared, can illuminate the lives of others. Just as Dr. Borges uses his musical gift to inspire and uplift, we too can find ways to share our talents, making the world a brighter, more connected place. Let us cherish and nurture these gifts, for they are the threads that weave the beautiful tapestry of our shared human experience.

Embrace the power of your unique gifts and let them flourish as you touch the lives of those around you. Whether through the gentle art of listening, the strength of leadership, or the warmth of hospitality, your contributions are invaluable. As we celebrate the diverse talents and passions that everyone brings to the table, we create a community rich with creativity, support, and love. Together, we can build a world where everyone feels seen, heard, and appreciated for the unique gifts they bring. We can inspire each other to shine brightly, recognizing that our shared journey benefits from the many talents we each contribute.

Devotional: The Maestro's Gift

Scripture: Psalm 33:3

"Sing unto him a new song; play skillfully with a loud noise."—Psalm 33:3

Devotional: The Maestro's Gift

Music possesses a wondrous ability to transcend mere words, forging a direct connection with the soul, especially when offered as a heartfelt gift of worship to the Lord. Psalm 33:3 beckons us to honor God with our talents, skillfully wielding the gifts bestowed upon us to illuminate His name with joy and glory. The maestro's unwavering dedication to his craft beautifully embodies this scripture, transforming each note into a resounding testament of faith and reverence.

With each stroke on the organ, he metamorphoses the church into a sanctuary of awe, uplifting spirits and guiding minds toward the boundless love and grace of God. This poignantly reminds us that our divinely given talents are not solely for our own benefit. The maestro's melodies become not merely sounds but vibrant reflections of God's presence, moving the congregation to worship with depth and joy.

Let us endeavor to wield our gifts in ways that serve others and honor God, recognizing that even the smallest offerings—when dedicated to Him—can illuminate the lives of those around us with light and hope.

Prayer:

Lord, we thank You for the gift of music and the talented hands that bring it to life. May we always recognize Your glory through the melodies that stir our hearts and awaken our spirits. Bless those who dedicate their talents to You, using them to lead others in worship and bring joy to the church. Inspire us, Lord, to use our gifts—whatever they may be—for Your glory and to bless those around us. May we always play skillfully, sing joyfully, and worship wholeheartedly. Amen.

Reflective Questions:

1. What gifts or talents do you possess, and how are you using them in God's kingdom?

2. Realizing that simply sharing our joy with others is a gift, could you share more of that this week with someone who may need a sympathetic shoulder?

4

THE RESURRECTION AND THE LIFE

The Rising Dawn

Charles E. Cravey

The stone rolled back, the dawn awoke,

The silent tomb, no longer spoke.

For He who triumphed over night,

Rose victor, radiant with light.

From shadows deep, the promise grew,

A life redeemed, a world made new.

Though thorns may pierce and storms assail,

The truth remains: His love prevails.

The cross was never end, but start—

A sacred vow, a beating heart.

The empty grave, a hope-filled sign,

Eternal love, divine design.

Oh, Resurrection! Oh, bright flame!

Through You, we bear His holy name.

Through loss, through pain, through fleeting breath,

In Christ, we conquer even death.

We all would like to live forever, wouldn't we? Those who live on in our hearts have immortality. They become timeless, etched into our memories and stories, shaping our lives long after they've departed. While physical immortality remains a fantasy, the legacy we leave behind is a testament to the lives we've touched. Through acts of kindness, wisdom shared, and love given freely, we achieve eternity. Our influence echoes through generations, like ripples in a pond, ensuring that we will always be present.

In this way, every moment of compassion and understanding we impart is like planting seeds in the garden of humanity, destined to bloom in the lives of those who follow us. We may not walk the earth forever, but our essence can thrive in the hearts we inspire and the dreams we nurture. By living with purpose and intent, we weave threads of connection that bind us to the future, transforming our finite existence into an everlasting presence.

The Bible speaks of immortality as a central theme throughout its texts. It provides insights into the concept of eternal life and the soul's existence beyond physical death. Various passages in the Bible discuss the idea of immortality, including the promise of everlasting life for those who believe in God and follow His commandments. The Bible also addresses the consequences of sin and the separation from God that leads to spiritual death. Through its teachings, the Bible offers comfort, guidance, and hope regarding the immortality of the soul and the promise of eternal life in the presence of God.

In world religions, the concept of immortality is a common belief across various faiths and belief systems. Many religions teach that there is eternal life beyond the physical existence on Earth. For example, in Christianity, followers believe in the promise of eternal life in Heaven after death. In Hinduism, the belief in reincarnation suggests that the soul is immortal and continues to be reborn until it achieves enlightenment and merges with the divine. Islamic followers similarly believe in an afterlife where the righteous will receive eternal paradise. The concept of immortality in world religions reflects the human desire for a continuation of existence beyond the limitations of mortal life.

In our sacred pursuit of immortality, it is essential that we illuminate each day as a radiant testament to what the Divine has destined us to be. By embracing an exemplary existence, we not only pay homage to our beliefs and values but also ignite inspiration within the hearts of others. This form of immortality transcends mere physical existence, weaving a legacy through our actions, words, and deeds. It is a spiritual immortality, flourishing through the profound impact we have on the world and the lives intertwined with ours. Thus, let us wholeheartedly dedicate ourselves to embodying the virtues and principles that resonate with our divine calling, ensuring our journey toward immortality is rich with purpose, meaning, and significance.

Within the tapestry of my mind live echoes of those from my past, their spirits weaving through my days. My eldest brother, Raymond, remains a steadfast guardian in my heart, ever present as he once was, shielding and guiding me in my youth. His essence lingers still, a cherished treasure etched in the fabric of my memories.

May we strive to live each day with integrity, kindness, and love, leaving an indelible mark on the tapestry of time. By nurturing the souls around us, we create a ripple effect that carries our essence forward, ensuring that our presence lingers long after we have departed. In this way, we become eternal, not in the flesh, but in the spirit and memories of those who continue to walk the path we once tread. Let our lives be a beacon of hope, a testament to the beauty of the human spirit, and a reflection of the divine within us all. As we journey through life, may we remain ever mindful of the footprints we leave behind, forever connected to the eternal cycle of life, love, and legacy.

Scripture:

John 11:25-26

"Jesus said unto her, I am the resurrection, and the life: he that believeth in me, though he were dead, yet shall he live: And whosoever liveth and believeth in me shall never die. Believest thou this?"

Devotional: The Resurrection and the Life

In John 11:25-26, Jesus offers comfort to Martha following the death of her brother Lazarus. He reveals a profound truth, declaring that He is not merely a bringer of life or resurrection, but that He Himself is the resurrection and the life. This revelation extends beyond physical restoration to convey the eternal hope that is found in Him. Belief in Jesus assures believers of everlasting life, even in the face of death.

The victory over death achieved by Jesus through His resurrection means that death no longer holds its fearful power, as He has triumphed over it. This truth emphasizes that through faith in Jesus, individuals enter an unbroken relationship with God that transcends even the grave. This knowledge of eternal hope and assurance is a beacon of light in life's darkest moments, providing comfort and strength. It prompts reflection on the depth of one's trust in Jesus as the ultimate source of life and hope, challenging individuals to confront any areas of doubt where His promise of eternal life could illuminate and bring peace.

Prayer:

Dear Heavenly Father,

Thank You for the gift of eternal life through Your Son, Jesus Christ. In a world that often feels fragile and uncertain, we cling to the hope that death is not the end. Help us live with confidence in Your promise and to share that hope with others who may feel lost or uncertain.

Strengthen our faith, Lord, and remind us daily that You are the resurrection and the life. May we walk boldly, knowing that nothing—not even death—can separate us from Your love.

In Jesus' name, we pray, Amen.

Reflection Questions

1. How does Jesus' promise of being the resurrection and the life impact the way you live your daily life?

2. Are there moments when it's hard to trust in His promises? How can you bring those doubts to Him?

3. How might you share this message of hope with someone who is struggling today?

5

I Can See Clearly Now - the Rain is Gone!

The Veil Lifted

Charles E. Cravey

I wandered once through shadowed ways,

Where doubts and fears obscured my gaze.

The storm clouds loomed, the path unclear,

Yet still, a whisper: Hope is near.

Then light broke forth, like morning's grace,

Illuming every darkened place.

The tears, like rain, were washed away,

A clearer vision claimed the day.

I see now through a lens of truth,

A joy reborn, the spring of youth.

The trials taught, the heart refined,

The beauty found in clearer mind.

Oh, every sorrow has its peace,

As storms depart, and burdens cease.

I walk now boldly, free of fear,

For light has shown—the way is here.

Challenges and tribulations are inherent in our existence. I fondly remember the story of legendary Babe Ruth, who once remarked that many failed to grasp the countless times he faced defeat at the plate; they only celebrated the soaring home runs! Yet, it was these very moments of struggle and perseverance that shaped him into an icon of resilience and determination. Life, much like the great game of baseball, is a series of pitches—some fast, some curving, and others impossible to hit. However, each swing, whether it results in a miss or a connection, teaches us something invaluable.

Embracing the storms and setbacks brings clarity, just as clouds part to reveal a brilliant sky. With every challenge faced, we gain wisdom and strength, allowing us to navigate life's journey with renewed optimism and hope. So, let us celebrate not only the triumphs but also the courage to face the trials, knowing that each step forward brings us closer to our dreams. In this grand journey, it's essential to remember that the true measure of success is not merely the destination but the experiences and growth we encounter along the way. Each setback is an opportunity to learn, adapt, and rise stronger than before. Just as Babe Ruth became a legend not only for his achievements but also for his ability to stand back up after each fall, we, too, can become the heroes of our own stories by embracing every challenge with grace and tenacity.

Let us cherish the rain as much as the sunshine, for together they create the vibrant tapestry of our lives. With each challenge conquered, we become more resilient, more understanding, and more capable of achieving the impossible. Here's to the journey ahead, with all its difficulties, and to the unwavering spirit within us that shines through the darkest of times.

Feeling defeated or discouraged? Then push on through the rain, for there's a beautiful rainbow on the other end awaiting you. God never puts more on us than we can handle.

Scripture:

Psalm 30:5

"For his anger endureth but a moment; in his favour is life: weeping may endure for a night, but joy cometh in the morning."

Devotional: Joy After the Storm

Life often resembles a tempest, with dark clouds of trials, uncertainties, and pain veiling our sight. Yet, the promise found in Psalm 30:5 whispers to our hearts, assuring us that these tribulations are but fleeting shadows. God's favor brings forth renewal, and His joy radiates like the dawn that follows a storm.

As we steadfastly navigate through life's challenges, placing our trust in God's provision, confusion gives way to clarity, turmoil transforms into peace, and sorrow blooms into joy. The "rain" that falls upon us is not everlasting—it cleanses our burdens, unveiling the glimmers of hope and purpose that God has woven into our existence.

Pause for a moment to ponder: Are there storms raging in your life while you await the skies to clear? Trust in God's perfect timing, for joy and clarity awaits just beyond the horizon. The morning shall arrive, bringing with it a renewed understanding of His boundless love and grace.

Prayer

Heavenly Father,

Thank you for being our shelter in the storm and our sunshine when the clouds part. Help us trust you through the rains of life, knowing that Your joy and clarity await us on the other side. Strengthen our faith as we navigate challenges and guide us toward the morning of hope and renewal.

May we always see Your hand at work, even in the downpour. We praise You for the joy that comes after sorrow and the peace that follows hardship.

In Jesus' name, Amen.

Reflective Questions:

1. What "storms" are you currently navigating, and how can you seek God's clarity during this time?

2. Have you experienced moments when joy came after a period of sorrow? How did you see God's hand in that process?

3. How can you encourage others who may feel stuck in their "rain" and help them look forward to the joy ahead?

6

THE WORLD IS CHANGING - RIGHT BEFORE YOUR EYES!

The Seasons Turn

Charles E. Cravey

The world is shifting, swift, and vast,
Each moment is new, the old recast.
Like whispers carried on the breeze,
Change dances lightly through the trees.

A season to plant, a season to reap,
A time for laughter, a time to weep.
With each turning tide, a chance to grow,
A divine masterpiece destined to show.

Though rain may fall, and skies may gray,
The dawn will herald a brighter day.
For every purpose beneath the sun,
Is woven by the Holy One.

So, embrace the change, let courage soar,
Perceive His touch through open door.
Though the earth may shift, God's love remains,
A steadfast anchor amidst life's chains.

Through every season, we find our place,
In the warmth of summer or winter's embrace.
Life's tapestry is rich and wide,
With moments shared and paths that collide.

In autumn's glow, we let go and release,
While spring's renewal brings us peace.
Each cycle a promise of hope and rebirth,
A testament to the beauty of Earth.

Let hearts be light, and spirits free,
In the dance of time, in harmony.
For as the seasons gently blend,
We find new beginnings in every end.

The world transforms with each fleeting moment, often unfolding right before our gaze. Who among us can truly keep pace with its wondrous evolution? Yet, in this dance of change, we find a rhythm that resonates deep within our souls. Each alteration, whether grand or subtle, offers an invitation to pause, reflect, and embrace the present. We are both witnesses and participants in this ever-evolving story, tasked with savoring each chapter as it unfolds.

The changing colors of the leaves and the lengthening or shortening days remind us of the beauty of impermanence. It is in this constant flow we uncover the true essence of life—resilient, vibrant, and endlessly surprising. So, let us cherish every transformation, knowing that each moment, no matter how brief, enriches the tapestry of our lives.

With each step forward, we weave our own threads into the fabric of time, creating patterns that reflect our journeys and dreams. The seasons, like wise old storytellers, whisper lessons of patience and grace, urging us to embrace the present with open hearts and minds. They teach us to find joy in the unexpected and strength in the gentle cycles of renewal.

Let us carry with us, as we walk through this world, the understanding that we should celebrate change, not fear it. It is the heartbeat of existence, the force that propels us toward new horizons and deeper connections. In the quiet moments between the hustle and bustle, may we find peace in knowing that we are part of something greater—a magnificent, ever-changing masterpiece that celebrates the beauty of life in all its forms.

In the end, it is not the destination that defines us, but the journey and how we choose to dance with the seasons of our lives.

Scripture:

Ecclesiastes 3:1

"To every thing there is a season, and a time to every purpose under the heaven:"

Devotional: Embracing Change with Faith

Change is one of life's unwavering certainties. In a realm that often feels like it's metamorphosing at an unprecedented pace—be it technologically, socially, or personally—it's all too easy to feel adrift. Yet, Ecclesiastes 3:1 gently reminds us that God's sovereign design imbues every season of existence, whether it is fraught with trials or filled with joy, with purpose.

As the world changes, we must adapt while holding firm to the unchanging truths of the Divine. He remains the same yesterday, today, and forevermore. When the tides of our circumstances rise and fall, His promises stand resolute, offering solace and direction. Each new season presents a wondrous opportunity for growth, a moment to realign with His divine purposes, and a chance to behold His hand at work.

Take heart knowing that, even as the world transforms, God reigns supreme. Trust in Him through the ebb and flow of life's seasons, allowing Him to guide you toward the destiny He has crafted for you.

Embrace the journey with faith, knowing that every experience shapes you into the person you become. When faced with uncertainty, remember that you are never alone; God walks with you, lighting your path with His love and wisdom.

In times of change, let courage be your companion and hope your guide. Seek the beauty in each moment, for even in challenges, there are lessons and blessings to uncover. As you navigate the ever-changing landscape of life, hold fast to the eternal truths that anchor your soul. Let them be your compass, directing you towards a life rich in purpose and fulfillment.

May you find peace knowing that every season holds meaning, and every step you take is part of a greater plan. With a heart open to His guidance, you can face any transition with strength and grace. Trust that the Creator of the universe is also the Author of your story, and He writes it with love and intention, crafting a narrative that is uniquely yours. So step boldly into the future, embracing each change as a gift, and rejoice in the unfolding journey that lies ahead.

Prayer:

Heavenly Father,

Amid the swirling tides of change, we find solace in Your steadfast presence. Thank you for being our unwavering anchor of strength and hope.

Grant us the grace to embrace the seasons of life with faith and courage, trusting that You weave all things together for our good.

When the shadows of uncertainty loom large, remind us of Your guiding hand and Your everlasting promises. May we grow in wisdom and discernment as we journey through this ever-shifting world.

In Jesus' name, Amen.

Reflective Questions:

1. How do you respond to change in your life? Are there areas where you struggle to trust God's plan?

2. What steps can you take to remain rooted in God's truth even as the world around you shifts?

3. How can you encourage others to embrace change with faith and hope in God's plan?

7

A Subtle Change

-—◆◈◆—-

The Subtle Change

Charles E. Cravey

Not every metamorphosis bursts forth with thunderous fame,
Some softly weave in, cloaked in gentle acclaim.
A tender sprout, kissed by dawn's warm grace,
A quiet ripple—a promise finds its place.

Despise not the hours when seeds lie in still repose,
For hidden grace flourishes, where the silent river flows.
In every whisper, within tranquility's palm,
God nurtures His pledges, a soothing balm.

Subtle transitions, both quiet and bright,
Reveal His love, unwavering in light.
Though fleeting moments may wear a soft guise,
His wondrous design shall ascend, shall rise.

In the dance of time, where shadows blend with light,
We find our strength in the whispers of the night.
Each gentle turn, each breath of serene air,
Carries the promise of His tender care.

In the tapestry of life, where threads entwine,
The smallest gestures are woven, divine.
A smile to a stranger, a hand reaching out,
In these simple acts, we find what life's about.

Hold fast to the truth that in silence, seeds grow,
In the stillness of moments, His presence we know.
For in the quiet, where the heart learns to see,
The grandeur of God's love sets us free.

So cherish the subtle, the meek, and the small,
For in these humble spaces, we hear His call.
Celebrate the beginnings, the soft-spoken ways,
And trust in the journey through all of your days.

In the quiet corners of our hearts and minds, these subtle changes weave a tapestry of hope and renewal. Like a painter with a delicate brush, each stroke, though small, adds depth and meaning to the canvas of our lives. We learn to treasure the gentle moments, the soft sighs of nature, and the tender exchanges that shape our journeys.

Through every season, as leaves turn and rivers flow, we find solace in the understanding that change does not always roar like a storm. It can be as muted as the setting sun, as serene as a child's laughter, or as profound as a silent prayer. In these moments, we remember the enduring beauty of life's simple gifts and the quiet strength in embracing change.

I stirred from slumber yesterday to find my yard still cloaked in the chill of winter's grasp. Yet, as late March dawned, I awoke to a whisper of transformation in the air. Overnight, the trees unfurled their tender buds, heralding the season's arrival! The azaleas unfurled their vibrant blooms. I spotted two bluebirds gracefully perching atop one of my bird boxes, affirming that spring had truly arrived.

The garden, once a tapestry of browns and greys, now burst with the promise of new beginnings. The sun, peeking over the horizon, cast a warm glow, gently coaxing the earth to awaken. Each delicate petal and leaf seemed to stretch toward the light, reveling in the renewed energy that the season brought.

In this quiet celebration of life, I paused to appreciate the subtle beauty that often goes unnoticed. The soft hum of bees busy at work, the gentle rustle of leaves in the breeze, and the cheerful song of the bluebirds filled the morning air with a symphony of hope. It was a reminder that even the most modest changes hold the power to uplift our spirits and fill our hearts with joy.

As I stood there, surrounded by nature's gentle revival, I felt a deep sense of gratitude for the resilience and grace that life offers. Spring, with its quiet persistence, had once again painted the world in vibrant hues, inviting us all to embrace the beauty of transformation.

Scripture:

Zechariah 4:10

"For who hath despised the day of small things? for they shall rejoice and shall see the plummet in the hand of Zerubbabel with those seven; they are the eyes of the LORD, which run to and fro through the whole earth."

Devotional: Celebrating Small Beginnings

Sometimes, the most transformative changes come in subtle, almost imperceptible ways. The scripture in Zechariah 4:10 reminds us not to overlook or despise the "small things." Small steps, small beginnings, and subtle shifts often pave the way for monumental growth. Just as a seed quietly takes root before growing into a mighty tree, God works through the little moments to bring about His grand purposes.

When we embrace subtle changes, trusting in God's guidance, we see His hand at work in the details. These changes might not make headlines, but they can transform hearts, situations, and lives in ways only God can orchestrate. Look for His fingerprints in the smallest acts of kindness, the quiet answers to prayer, and the gentle nudges toward His path.

Prayer:

Heavenly Father,

We express our gratitude for the exquisite beauty nestled within the tiniest changes and new beginnings. Illuminate our hearts to recognize Your divine craftsmanship in every detail and grant us the faith to embrace Your impeccable timing as You weave growth and transformation into our lives. May we remain ever mindful of the "small things" You employ to mold our existence and the world we inhabit.

Guide us in patience and steadfast belief as we await the fulfillment of Your promises. Let these gentle shifts inspire us to draw nearer to You, ever aware that You are tirelessly working for our ultimate good.

In Jesus' name, Amen.

Reflective Questions:

Reflect on the moments of subtle change in your life. How has God used those to draw you closer to Him or to fulfill His purposes?

1. Could you recall a moment of subtle change in your life that led to significant growth or transformation?

2. Why do you think it's sometimes difficult to value small beginnings or quiet progress?

3. How can you remind yourself—and others—that God works powerfully even through subtle shifts and "small things"?

8

WHEN THE TEMPESTS RAGE

Steadfast in the Storm

Charles E. Cravey

The winds may wail, the waves may swell,
As tempests cast their shadowed spell.
Yet within my heart, a song will rise,
For God is near—my unwavering prize.

Through roaring seas, I shall take my stand,
Supported by His mighty hand.
Though flames may dance, and their heat may bite,
I'll find refuge beneath His light.

No storm can shatter what He protects.
No trial can conquer His effects.
In His embrace, my spirit stays,
Through every tempest, His grace ablaze.

This poem, a heartfelt reflection, captures the essence of finding solace and strength in faith amidst life's tumultuous moments. It resonates deeply, much like the tale of our night at sea, where courage and companionship guided us through adversity. In both the poem and our shared experience, the theme of inner resilience shines brightly, reminding us of the enduring power of hope and trust. As we navigate the unpredictable waters of life, such reflections embolden us, encouraging a steadfast spirit and an open heart.

Upon the azure expanse off the coast of Belize, I found myself ensnared in my inaugural, and most prolonged, chill-laden night of fishing. Beyond the discomfort that wrapped around us like a shroud, our solitary prize was a formidable 32-pound red snapper, caught with a dragline. Anchored far from the comforting embrace of the shore, a storm swept in, and the surging waves transformed our modest 20-foot vessel into a mere plaything of the tempest. For over an hour, the storm raged, and our crew grew weary, yearning for the safety of land. An unsettling thought flickered through my mind: what would I do if our boat succumbed to the depths? I felt trepidation in that moment, but God's embrace comforted me.

To this day, my friends and I recount that experience, reflecting on the trials it presented to each of us. Life, much like the sea, can conjure tempests when we least expect them. But it is in these moments of adversity that we often discover our true strength and resilience. The storm, while fierce, taught us invaluable lessons about teamwork, trust, and the indomitable spirit of human perseverance.

As the clouds eventually parted and the first light of dawn touched the horizon, the sea calmed, leaving us with a profound sense of gratitude and a renewed appreciation for the beauty and unpredictability of nature. We navigated back to shore, our hearts lighter and our bonds stronger, having faced the storm together.

Now, whenever I look out over the ocean, I am reminded of that night—a testament to the unpredictability of life and the courage it takes to weather its storms. It's a memory that continues to inspire me, encouraging me to embrace challenges with an open heart and a steadfast spirit.

Scripture:

Isaiah 43:2

"When thou passest through the waters, I will be with thee; and through the rivers, they shall not overflow thee: when thou walkest through the fire, thou shalt not be burned; neither shall the flame kindle upon thee."

Devotional: Anchored in the Storm

Life's tempests often descend upon us unannounced—unexpected trials, heartaches, and fears that loom large, threatening to engulf our spirits. Yet, Isaiah 43:2 extends a radiant promise: we are never alone, even amidst the fiercest storms. God's presence remains steadfast. His might surpasses the tumultuous waters and searing flames that may appear insurmountable.

This verse does not guarantee the absence of storms but assures us of divine protection as we navigate through them. The rivers shall not drown us, nor shall the flames consume us. Instead, God employs these challenges to fortify our faith and refine our character, drawing us ever closer to Him.

When the tempests swirl in your life, hold fast to the knowledge that your anchor is secure. Trust in the One who walks alongside you, who calms the raging storms, and who promises that no wave or fire shall sever the bond of His love. In those moments of uncertainty, let the assurance of His presence buoy your heart. He is the lighthouse guiding you safely to shore, the gentle whisper in the wind that reminds you of His unfailing promise. Allow your spirit to rest in the comfort of His grace, knowing that each trial is but a steppingstone toward deeper faith and understanding.

As you journey through life's unpredictable seas, remember that every storm is an opportunity to witness His strength and to marvel at the depth of His care. Embrace the challenges with courage, knowing that you are never alone. With each wave, with each gust of wind, you are being shaped and molded into a testament to His enduring love and faithfulness.

May your heart remain open and your spirit steadfast, ever ready to face the storms with the confidence that comes from being anchored in His eternal embrace. Let this truth illuminate your path, bringing peace and hope amidst the darkest nights and the wildest seas.

Prayer:

Heavenly Father,

When life's storms rage and fears surround us, we find peace in Your presence. Thank you for the promise that you walk with us through the waters and shield us from the flames. Strengthen our faith when we feel weak and remind us of Your unshakable love in every trial. Help us trust you completely, knowing that you are our anchor in every tempest. Use the storms we face to draw us closer to you and to reveal your glory through our lives.

In Jesus' name, Amen.

Reflective Questions:

1. What storms are you currently facing, and how can you anchor yourself in God's promises during this time?

2. Reflect on a past trial where God carried you through. How can that memory strengthen your faith for today?

9

As We Grow Older

What Happens When Aging

Charles E. Cravey

Six pills in the morning, another five at night.

You would think I was dying, and you might be right!

Day after day, life gets harder to bear.

I'm losing my memory and also my hair.

It's up at 5:30, come rain or come shine.

Some days I feel like I'm losing my mind.

But deep in my heart, there's a flicker of light,

A stubborn resolve that continues to fight.

Though weary and worn, I'm still here to say,

Each sunrise whispers, "You've made it today."

The road may be rugged, the climb steep and tall,

But even when stumbling, I'm refusing to fall.

For life, though it's fragile, still holds its own charm,

In laughter, in moments, in love's charming arm.

So I'll take these pills and face every test,

With hope in my soul and strength in my chest.

For while the days may feel heavy with strife,

I'll savor the beauty in this precious life.

Boy, did the years sneak up on me like a slow, slithering snake in the grass! I turned around the other day, looked at myself in the mirror, and realized that seventy-four is what I used to refer to as "ancient." Now, I guess I'm a relic, but I refuse to let it take over my life. I have a lot of things to do before the end of this journey. As I reflect on the passage of time, I am filled with a sense of urgency to make the most of every moment. Despite the wrinkles and gray hairs, I am determined to embrace the wisdom and experience that comes with age. There are still dreams to chase, adventures to embark on, and memories to create. I refuse to be defined by a number; instead, I choose to live each day to the fullest, savoring the beauty of life in all its forms.

My persistent aches and pains result from numerous surgeries. Each surgical procedure has left its mark on my body, resulting in varying levels of discomfort and physical limitations. Despite the medical interventions aimed at improving my health, the aftermath of these surgeries has led to a chronic condition that affects my daily life.

Over the years, I have had to undergo several surgeries for different health issues. From minor procedures to major operations, each surgery has taken a toll on my body. The healing process post-surgery has been challenging, often accompanied by pain and discomfort. The cumulative effect of these surgeries has contributed to the chronic aches and pains that I now endure regularly.

These surgeries impact more than just physical pain. The significant mental and emotional strain comes from coping with the aftermath of multiple surgeries. Patience and resilience have been required during the long and arduous recovery process. The constant battle with pain has affected my quality of life and daily activities, making simple tasks more challenging.

Despite facing the prospect of undergoing surgery, I refuse to let it define me as a victim. Instead, I choose to rise above it, just as I have done in the past. My determination to persevere remains unwavering, and I am committed to continuing my life's work of writing for you, dear reader. Together, we can navigate through this challenging phase of our lives, emerging stronger and more resilient. Let our shared journey inspire hope and resilience in each other as we embrace the power of words and faith in God to overcome adversity.

Scripture:

2 Corinthians 4:16

"For which cause we faint not; but though our outward man perish, yet the inward man is renewed day by day."

Devotional: Grace in Every Season

Aging is an inevitable part of life, and with it comes physical changes that can sometimes feel discouraging. However, the Bible offers us a beautiful perspective: while the "outward man" may grow weaker, the "inward man" is being renewed daily. This renewal is not just a promise—it's a testament to the grace and faithfulness of God as He works in and through us in every season.

Aging brings wisdom, depth, and the opportunity to draw nearer to the Lord. With every year, we grow richer in faith, experience, and understanding of His love. The world may focus on youth and outward beauty, but God values the enduring beauty of a spirit refined by time and trust in Him.

Take heart that aging is not just a fading of the body but a blossoming of the soul. In His hands, every wrinkle, every gray hair, and every moment carries purpose and glory.

Prayer

Dear Heavenly Father,

Thank you for the gift of life and the journey of aging. Help us embrace the changes that come with time, trusting in Your promise of daily renewal. May we find joy in the wisdom and grace You give in every season of life.

Teach us to see aging not as a loss but as a deeper walk with You—a time to treasure Your love and reflect Your glory. Renew our hearts daily and draw us closer to You so that we may live with purpose, peace, and joy all our days.

In Jesus' name, Amen.

Reflective Questions:

1. How do you view aging in your life? Does it encourage or challenge your faith?

2. In what ways have you experienced God's renewal of your "inward man" as the years pass?

3. How can you honor and encourage others on their own journeys of aging, offering God's perspective of grace   and beauty?

10

"Pruning is Necessary"

"The Gardener's Touch"

Charles E. Cravey

The Gardener comes with hands so wise,

To tend the vine beneath the skies.

With care, He prunes; with love, He trims.

To strengthen branches, frail and dim.

Each cut may sting, each loss may ache,

Yet beauty blooms for His Name's sake.

Through seasons harsh, through winds that blow,

New life takes root; new fruit will grow.

The vine that yields must first let go,

Of withered leaves and husks below.

Though pain may linger, trust His art,

For pruning shapes the fruitful heart.

His shears refine, His hands restore,

Our lives transformed to bear much more.

So yield to Him, the Gardener's will,

And watch His purpose be fulfilled.

Every year, Renee and I meticulously prune our azaleas, blueberries, shrubs, camellias, and other plants to keep them healthy. This annual pruning routine is crucial for promoting growth, maintaining shape, and preventing diseases. We dedicate time to trim away dead or overgrown branches carefully, improving air circulation and sunlight exposure for the plants. Despite the abundance of plants requiring pruning, we find joy and fulfillment in our roles as dedicated gardeners. We understand that neglecting this essential process will cause the plants to deteriorate, leading to a haggard appearance and potential death. By prioritizing regular pruning, we ensure the longevity and vitality of our beloved garden.

Similarly, God shapes our lives for the benefit of our spiritual growth. Just as a potter molds clay into a beautiful vessel, God carefully crafts our experiences, challenges, and blessings to shape us into the individuals He created us to be. Through both trials and triumphs, God works in mysterious ways to guide us along the path of spiritual development and enlightenment. Trusting in His plan and surrendering to His will allows us to grow in faith, wisdom, and understanding. Just as a sculptor chisels away at a block of marble to reveal the masterpiece within, God's handiwork in our lives reveals the beauty and purpose He has designed for each of us.

Scripture:

John 15:2

"Every branch in me that beareth not fruit he taketh away: and every branch that beareth fruit, he purgeth it, that it may bring forth more fruit."

Devotional: "Pruning is Necessary"

"Pruning is necessary"—a statement encompassing both hardship and hope. John 15:2 compares us to branches on a vine cared for by God, the Master Gardener. We should not view pruning as punishment.

Letting go of relationships, habits, and pursuits not aligned with God's will is life's pruning. This might involve facing challenges that test our faith while building our character. Although the process may be difficult or painful, the Gardener's touch is always gentle, precise, and loving.

Pruning prepares us for greater fruitfulness. It's through this refining process we grow closer to God, bear more of His likeness, and fulfill His purposes. Trust in the Gardener's wisdom, knowing that every cut brings forth something beautiful.

Where will God's pruning affect your life today?

Prayer:

Dear Heavenly Father,

Thank you for your wise and caring guidance in our lives. Despite the challenges of pruning, we have faith in Your perfect love and plan. We need to remove anything hindering our growth to enable us to bear fruit that glorifies You. Help us submit to Your plan, trusting that each step benefits us. In Jesus' name, Amen.

Reflective Questions:

1. Could you identify areas in your life where God might be "pruning" you for greater fruitfulness?

2. How do you typically respond when you face challenges or need to let go of something?

3. What fruit has come from a season of pruning in your past, and how did it shape your faith?

11

STANDING ON THE PROMISES

Standing on the Promises

Charles E. Cravey

Upon this rock, unmoved, I stand,

Securely held by the Father's hand.

His promises, a steadfast shore,

Through trials faced forevermore.

When shadows creep and fears arise,

His Word brings light to the darkest skies.

A covenant sealed, unbroken, strong,

A melody—my heart's pure song.

Storms may rage and tempests roll.

Yet peace abides within my soul.

For every step, His voice assures,

Each promise speaks. His love endures.

No weight of doubt, no earthly foe,

Can shake the truths I've come to know.

In His promises, firm and sure,

My faith will rest, my hope secure.

Since my childhood days, I have cherished the hymn "Standing on the Promises." This timeless hymn has been a staple in churches for as long as I can remember. Its message is powerful and clear, reminding us to stand firm on the promises of God, even in times of uncertainty and doubt.

In times of uncertainty and doubt, we can find solace in the promises made to us. These promises serve as a beacon of hope, guiding us through challenges and reminding us of the unwavering support that is always available to us. Whether it is the promise of love, forgiveness, or protection, we can find comfort in knowing that we are not alone. The knowledge that God loves us empowers us to confront any challenge. Let us hold on to these promises tightly, allowing them to light our way and lead us to a place of peace and fulfillment.

Scripture:

2 Corinthians 1:20

"For all the promises of God in him are yea, and in him Amen, unto the glory of God by us."

Devotional: "Unshaken Faith in His Promises"

Every promise contained within the sacred scriptures serves as a testament to, and a genuine reflection of, the unwavering and immutable nature of God's character. 2 Corinthians 1:20 powerfully reminds us that Christ fulfills every promise, so we should base our assurance not on our abilities but on His unchanging Word. When life's uncertainties tug at our resolve, we can stand firm, knowing His power guarantees His promises.

To stand firm on God's promises causes an unwavering faith, a faith that endures even amidst life's tumultuous storms, those trials that challenge our resolve and test our limits to the utmost. However, we can remain steadfast, securely knowing that His boundless power and unwavering love eternally guarantee His promises to sustain us through the toughest times. Because His promises are both "yes" and "amen," they are not only true but also eternally enduring, providing a steadfast and everlasting foundation for all those who place their faith in Him. As you stand firmly on the promises of God, are you prepared to allow His Word to shape and direct your faith and path, guiding you through life's journey?

Prayer:

Faithful Father,

Thank You for Your Word, which speaks life and assurance to my soul. Teach me to trust in the promises You have given and help me stand firm even when life challenges my faith. Thank You for fulfilling Your promises through Christ and making them unshakable and eternal. May I honor You by living out Your truth and standing boldly on Your Word.

In Jesus' name, Amen.

Reflective Questions:

1. Which promise of God has brought you the most encouragement in your life?

2. How can you apply His promises to the current challenges you are facing?

3. Are there areas of your life where doubts about His promises still linger? How can you address them?

12

The Guiding Light of His Presence

"Lighthouse of Grace"

Charles E. Cravey

Above the roar of the restless tide,

A light beams clear, a place to abide.

Through storm-clad skies and waves that break,

It whispers hope for weary's sake.

The ocean's anger, wild and loud,

Cannot obscure the Love avowed.

A tower stands, steadfast, secure,

A guiding grace, steadfast and pure.

Fear may rise and courage wane,

Yet the light remains through every strain.

A gentle call in the tempest's face,

"Come, find rest in My embrace."

When shadows fall, and paths seem dim,

Lift your eyes; fix them on Him.

For in His light, we find our way,

Through night's dark grip, to dawn's new day.

Since my childhood, the old church hymn, "Just a Little Talk with Jesus," has held a special place in my heart and continues to resonate with me. The hymn's lyrics describe the power of prayer and the comfort of talking with Jesus. This song has been a source of strength and solace for me during challenging times, reminding me of the importance of faith and a higher power in my life. The melody and message of "Just a Little Talk with Jesus" have become a cherished part of my spiritual journey, offering me a sense of peace and connection to my beliefs.

While the hymn may no longer make it in the agenda of most major churches, small churches still sing its wondrous words and receive its blessings. The tradition of hymn-singing holds a special place in the hearts of many congregations, offering a sense of connection to the past and fostering a deep spiritual experience. Despite changes in worship styles and music preferences, hymns continue to resonate with believers in small churches, providing a source of comfort, inspiration, and unity.

Hymns are more than just songs; they are powerful expressions of faith that have stood the test of time. In small churches, where the sense of community is strong and traditions are cherished, hymns play a significant role in worship services. Generations pass down these timeless melodies and lyrics, creating a sense of continuity and shared heritage among church members.

The act of singing hymns together fosters a sense of unity and togetherness within the congregation. Whether it's a familiar favorite or a new discovery, hymns can bring people together in worship, creating a sacred space where believers can come together to praise and glorify God.

May I ask a personal question from this hymn? Have you had a little talk with the master of all creation lately? At what level is your spiritual temperature? Perhaps today is the day to get back in touch with the Master of your soul.

In our busy lives, it is easy to lose touch with our spiritual connection and the deeper aspects of our being. Having a conversation with the divine, whether through prayer, meditation, or reflection, can help realign our spiritual temperature and bring peace to our souls.

Let us take a moment today to pause, reflect, and reconnect with the Master of all creation. In doing so, we may find guidance, comfort, and a renewed sense of purpose in our journey of faith.

Scripture:

Isaiah 41:10

"Fear thou not; for I am with thee: be not dismayed; for I am thy God: I will strengthen thee; yea, I will help thee; yea, I will uphold thee with the right hand of my righteousness."

Devotional: "The Guiding Light of His Presence"

Life often feels like navigating uncharted waters—waves of uncertainty rise, winds of fear howl, and darkness clouds our vision. In moments like these, God's presence becomes our unshakable lighthouse, steadfast and unwavering. Isaiah 41:10 reminds us we don't have to face the storm alone. His promise to strengthen and uphold us is not just comforting; it's a call to trust, even when we can't see the shoreline.

The lighthouse doesn't calm the storm, nor does it promise a swift journey. Instead, it provides clarity and direction, reminding us of where safety lies. God guides us in the same way—He may not remove our challenges, but He ensures we never lose our way. His light cuts through the chaos, drawing us nearer to His refuge. The question is, will you keep your eyes fixed on His light, trusting His steady hand, or will the distractions of the storm pull your gaze away?

Prayer:

Heavenly Father,

I am eternally grateful for your presence as a guiding light that illuminated my path through the darkest hours of my life. When my strength fails and I am weakened, I ask for your support to help me regain my strength. I ask for the guidance to trust in Your direction, even when the path ahead is unclear and uncertain, and I pray I learn to have faith in your guidance. May the entirety of my life serve as a testament, a living example, to the unwavering safety and boundless hope that is inherent in your constant and unfailing care.

In Jesus' name, Amen.

Reflective Questions:

1. When have you felt God's guidance in a difficult situation?

2. How can you remind yourself of His promises when fear begins to creep in?

3. Are there areas of your life where you're struggling to trust His direction?

13

A SPIRITUAL FORK IN THE ROAD

A Spiritual Fork in the Road

Charles E. Cravey

Two paths before me, winding, vast,

Each choice a shadow of the past.

One calls my heart to fleeting ease,

The other whispers, "Follow Me, please."

The road of self is wide and bright,

Yet fades to darkness, void of light.

The narrow way is steep, unknown,

Yet leads me to His promised throne.

At this fork, my soul must choose,

Eternal gain or temporal ruse.

With trembling heart, I lift my prayer,

"Lord, guide me to Your perfect care."

We each make tremendous choices every day. From deciding what to buy at the grocery store based on our dietary preferences and budget to selecting what to wear to work based on the weather and dress code, choices are an integral part of our daily lives. These decisions, no matter how seemingly insignificant, shape our experiences and reflect our values and priorities. Whether it's choosing between organic and conventional produce or deciding between a formal suit and business casual attire, each choice contributes to the tapestry of our lives. The accumulation of these daily choices forms the intricate landscape of our existence, highlighting our individuality and the complexity of our decision-making processes.

In life, we often stand at a crossroads, faced with important decisions that will shape our future. Not only are these decisions significant in terms of our physical and material well-being, but they also carry profound spiritual implications. The choices we make at these junctures can have a lasting impact on our lives and the lives of those around us.

At these crossroads, our values, beliefs, and aspirations force us to confront them. We must weigh the options before us, considering not only the short-term consequences but also the long-term effects of our decisions. These moments of choice are pivotal, representing opportunities for growth, transformation, and self-discovery. During these times, we face genuine tests and challenges, requiring us to listen to our inner voice and follow the path aligned with our true selves.

The crossroads of life present us with the greatest choices we will ever make. They require courage, wisdom, and discernment to navigate successfully. As we stand at these spiritual crossroads, let us embrace the opportunity for growth and choose the path that leads us towards our highest good.

Scripture:

Matthew 7:13-14

"Enter ye in at the strait gate: for wide is the gate, and broad is the way, that leadeth to destruction, and many there be which go in thereat: Because strait is the gate, and narrow is the way, which leadeth unto life, and few there be that find it."

Devotional: "Choosing the Right Path"

Life is full of crossroads, moments where we must choose between paths that shape our spiritual journey. Matthew 7:13-14 speaks to this universal experience, contrasting the wide gate and broad way with the strait gate and narrow way.

The wide path may seem appealing—its ease, popularity, and worldly allure draw many. Yet, it leads to destruction, pulling us further from the life God has called us to live. The narrow way, though challenging and less traveled, brings us closer to Him. It requires sacrifice, faith, and trust in His guidance.

When faced with a spiritual fork in the road, the choice becomes a test of commitment. Do we rely on fleeting comforts, or do we surrender to His will, trusting Him to lead us toward eternal life? Remember, God's path may not always be the easiest, but it is always the best. Which path will you take today?

Prayer:

Heavenly Father, Thank You for guiding me through life's many crossroads. When I stand at spiritual forks in the road, help me choose the narrow way that leads to You. Strengthen me to resist the pull of worldly distractions and give me courage to follow Your will, even when the path seems difficult. May my steps honor You and lead me closer to Your light.

In Jesus' name, Amen.

Reflective Questions:

1. Could you recall a time when you faced a spiritual fork in the road? What did you learn from that experience?

2. What are some practical ways to discern God's will when making life decisions?

3. What fears or doubts may be preventing you from taking the narrow way in certain areas of your life?

14

STREAMS IN THE DESERT

Streams in the Desert

Charles E. Cravey

Beneath the sun's relentless blaze,
Where barren sands stretch endless ways,
A muted stream begins to flow,
God's promise speaks where hope feels low.

Its waters quench the weary soul,
Restore the heart and make it whole.
Through wilderness, His love will gleam,
A desert turned to verdant dream.

The dunes may shift, the winds may rise,
And doubts may darken clouded skies.
Yet through it all, His hand prevails,
A steady guide when strength seems frail.

No parched terrain, no barren field,
Can stand against what God will yield.
For every thirst, His streams provide,
A flood of grace, a wellspring wide.

So when the desert paths extend,
And trials test where roads may end,
Lift up your eyes, behold His way,
His streams of mercy flood the day.

With every step, let faith take hold,
Trust in His Word, more precious than gold.
In desert lands, His promise stays,
A river of life through endless days.

The old saying, "When you get to the end of your rope, tie a knot and hang on; help is on its way," is so true many times in life. God gives each of us a proverbial rope to pull us through moments of peril or indecision. This saying emphasizes the importance of perseverance and resilience in the face of challenges. It suggests that even when we feel like we have reached our limit, there is always a way to hold on and find a solution.

In times of adversity, much like how a rope can serve as a lifeline, our faith and determination can act as guiding forces to help us navigate through challenging situations. This powerful metaphor underscores the idea that, even when faced with insurmountable obstacles, there is always a glimmer of hope and support within reach. Just as a rope can provide stability and a way forward in times of crisis, our unwavering belief in ourselves and our ability to persevere can lead us towards brighter horizons. This analogy serves as a poignant reminder that, with faith and determination, we can overcome obstacles and emerge stronger on the other side.

Scripture:

Isaiah 43:19 (KJV):

"Behold, I will do a new thing; now it shall spring forth; shall ye not know it? I will even make a way in the wilderness, and rivers in the desert."

Devotional: *"Streams in the Desert"*

Deserts are often symbols of difficulty—a place where life struggles to survive, and hope feels distant. Yet, Isaiah 43:19 reveals a promise that defies natural expectations: God creates rivers in the desert, making a way in what seems impassable.

These streams are a reminder of His divine provision. In seasons of spiritual dryness, when challenges appear insurmountable, God offers refreshment. Just as He brought water from a rock for the Israelites, He transforms barren places in our lives into sources of restoration.

Are you walking through a desert season today? Trust in God's ability to bring streams of renewal—whether through His Word, His Spirit, or the people He places in your life. Your current hardships may feel overwhelming, but with God, the desert becomes a testimony of His miraculous power.

Prayer:

Gracious Lord,

Your generosity and compassion have brought light into my darkest moments, and for that, I offer my sincerest thanks. In moments of exhaustion and depletion, please help me remember that your presence is a wellspring of revitalization and restoration, offering me renewed energy and hope. I pray you will teach me to trust in your promises, even when the path ahead seems insurmountable and incredibly difficult to navigate. Grant me the peace of mind that comes from knowing that Your provision is sufficient and that You have the power to transform even the most barren aspects of my life into vibrant, fruitful landscapes.

In Jesus' name, Amen.

Reflective Questions:

1. Have you ever experienced God's provision during a "desert season" in your life?

2. What steps can you take to trust in His ability to create streams in your wilderness?

3. How can you encourage others facing difficult times?

15

THE POTTER'S HANDS

The Potter's Hands

Charles E. Cravey

A lump of clay, so rough, unformed,
By Potter's hands is gently warmed.
With every touch, a shape appears,
A vessel born through love and tears.

The wheel may spin, the pressure rise,
Yet through it all, the Potter tries.
To mold, to carve, to craft with care,
A masterpiece beyond compare.

Though cracks may form and flaws be found,
The Potter's grace will still abound.
He mends the breaks, refines the lines,
And in His work, His glory shines.

Surrender, clay, to shaping's call.
For in His hands, you're made for all.
A purpose great, divinely planned,
Fulfilled within the Potter's hands.

During our vacation to the stunning North Carolina mountains, we had the pleasure of visiting a local potter's shed with our friends, where we watched him show his creative and skillful work. The potter's skillful hands and fingers mesmerized me as they transformed a simple mound of clay into a beautiful vase, a truly captivating display of artistry. Glancing to his left, I observed a significant quantity of broken pottery, from which I could deduce its point of origin. He explained that he'd rejected those shards from his earlier work. He would melt down those materials and repurpose them for a different project.

The comparison between our lives and the Potter's Shed came to mind, highlighting the similarities and the transformative nature of both. Every day, we are in God's hands, being carefully shaped and formed by Him, and it is His divine will that determines our ultimate being. However, when we forsake His abundant love, mercy, and grace in favor of our own self-interests, we shatter into fragments, losing our wholeness and integrity.

Remember: we are clay in the master Potter's hands and are being shaped daily into the person God wants us to be. Yield to the Master.

Scripture:

Jeremiah 18:6 (KJV):

"O house of Israel, cannot I do with you as this potter? saith the LORD. Behold, as the clay is in the potter's hand, so are ye in mine hand, O house of Israel."

Devotional: *"Shaped by the Master"*

In the hands of the Potter, we find our identity. Jeremiah 18:6 paints a vivid picture of God's sovereignty and care. As clay in His hands, we are being shaped, refined, and prepared for His purpose. The process, however, is not always easy. The potter's work may involve pressure, reshaping, or even starting anew.

His love guides every spin of the wheel and every touch of His hand. He sees not just the flaws and cracks, but the potential for beauty and purpose. When we surrender fully to His shaping, we allow His divine artistry to transform us into vessels fit for His glory.

Are you willing to trust the Potter, even when the shaping feels uncomfortable? Remember, he still has work to do with you. The hands that hold you are the same hands that created the universe—strong, purposeful, and full of grace.

Prayer:

Father God,
With complete trust and confidence, I humbly submit myself to the expertise and skill of your capable hands. Even when the process of transformation is difficult, mold me into the person You have called me to be, shaping me and guiding me in Your plan for my life. I would like to learn to trust in Your wisdom and to accept the changes that You bring into my life with open arms. I am grateful for your belief in my abilities, even with my flaws and shortcomings. As the clay in Your hands, Master Potter, may my life bring You glory and honor.

In Jesus' name, Amen.

Reflective Questions:

1. Are there areas of your life where you feel God is reshaping you? How are you responding to that process?

2. How can you find peace in knowing that God is working on you, even when you don't understand His methods?

3. What would it look like to fully surrender to the Potter's hands in your daily life?

16

SOCIAL SECURITY

"Eternal Security"

Charles E. Cravey

Beneath the heavens, strong and wide,

Dwells a love in which we can abide.

Not built by hands or by decree,

But etched in grace, eternally free.

Through life's sharp turns and valleys deep,

Our Shepherd promises our souls to keep.

No storm too fierce, no night too long,

For in His arms, we are secure and strong.

The world may falter, systems may fail,

Yet His steadfast mercy will always prevail.

The anchor that holds when the tempest grows,

The Rock is unyielding, the refuge we know.

When doubts arise and fears take flight,

His Word remains our guiding light.

No power on earth, no scheme, no snare,

Can pluck us from His tender care.

In muted streams or shadows, dim,

We place our trust, our all, in Him.

For every moment, through joy or strife,

He guards our steps, sustaining life.

So, rest, dear soul, in His embrace,

Where peace flows freely, a boundless grace.

Our "social security" is found above,

Rooted in His everlasting love.

Social Security deeply divides Americans. This government program, established in 1935, provides financial support to retired workers, individuals with disabilities, and families of deceased workers. Critics argue that Social Security's financial unsustainability and discouragement of personal responsibility cause its elimination. However, others depend on it for vital income and financial security. The debate over the future of Social

Security reflects differing views on the role of government in ensuring the well-being of its citizens and the challenges of addressing an aging population and changing economic landscape.

The future of Social Security remains uncertain, with ongoing debates and reforms. However, amidst this uncertainty, a different security exists—spiritual, social security. This form of security stems from a belief in a higher power and the assurance that everything is under divine control. In times of need, this spiritual security serves as a steadfast foundation, offering unwavering support and guidance.

When we turn to spiritual social security, we find solace in the belief that God has everything under control. Unlike earthly systems that may falter or deplete, God's assistance is boundless and everlasting. His grace acts as a safety net, always ready to lift us up and lead us back to Him. This assurance of divine support provides comfort in times of uncertainty and serves as a constant reminder that we are never alone.

In the realm of spiritual social security, the unchanging nature of God's love and grace ensures a sense of stability and peace. Regardless of what may happen to earthly systems, we can find reassurance knowing that God's assistance is infinite, and His grace is always available to guide us through life's challenges. This security enables us to navigate uncertainty with faith and courage, knowing that God holds us.

Scripture:

Psalm 121:7-8

"The LORD shall preserve thee from all evil: he shall preserve thy soul. The LORD shall preserve thy going out and thy coming in from this time forth, and even for evermore."

Devotional: "God's Security"

The term "social security" often suggests a system designed to ensure financial stability. Yet, we find our greatest security not in checks, policies, or provisions, but in God's unchanging love and care for us.

Psalm 121 reminds us that God is not a distant observer but an intimate guardian who watches over every aspect of our lives. His watchfulness transcends circumstances, providing security that no earthly system can replicate.

In moments when we feel shaken—whether by financial hardship, illness, or personal challenges—this truth anchors us: God's care is constant, His protection unwavering, and His provisions limitless. True security doesn't depend on what we have or achieve; our ultimate "social security" rests in knowing that He holds our comings and goings, both now and forevermore.

Prayer:

Dear Heavenly Father,

We offer our sincerest gratitude for your unwavering protection and provision throughout all our time together. In times of uncertainty and looming fear, we implore You to remind us of Your unwavering and faithful care for us. We implore You, guide us to place our faith not in the transient structures of this world, but in the steadfast and immutable essence of Your divine being. Let comfort and peace come to us, knowing You hold our lives securely in Your divine hands.

In Jesus' name, Amen.

Reflective Questions:

1. How do you define "security" in your life? Is it more tied to earthly

systems or your faith in God?

2. Could you recall a time when God's care provided for you unexpectedly? How did that experience deepen your trust in Him?

3. What steps can you take this week to trust God more in areas where you feel uncertain or insecure?

17

THE INTERSECTION OF BELIEF AND REALITY

"Where Belief Meets the Real"

Charles E. Cravey

Faith's gentle whispers, unseen yet clear,

Guiding each step through doubt and fear.

Not just a dream, not a distant tale,

But strength that anchors when storms assail.

In the muted dawn and the day's demands,

God's truth extends, shaping our hands.

Belief transcends what eyes can perceive,

Turning hopes into truths we achieve.

Reality bends to the heart that trusts,

As heaven ignites the earthbound dust.

Where belief and reality intertwine,

God's promises unfold, divine.

Through shadows that linger, where fears reside,

Faith leads the way, our unseen guide.

Each prayer a torch in the darkest night,

Transforming despair into radiant light.

When mountains loom and valleys stretch wide,

Faith gives the strength to stand and stride.

Not a fleeting thought, but a steadfast flame,

That reshapes the world in God's name.

Belief breathes life into dreams untold,

Turning the ordinary into pure gold.

A meeting place of hope and sight,

Where faith reveals eternal light.

So, trust in the One who makes all things new,

Who bridges the gap between what's seen and true.

In Him, belief, and reality embrace,

A reflection of His boundless grace.

When delving into the distinction between what we believe and true reality, our perceptions and beliefs may not always align with objective truth. Beliefs are subjective and personal convictions that a multitude of factors can influence, such as upbringing, culture, experiences, and emotions. True reality refers to the actual state of things independent of our thoughts or beliefs. This discrepancy between belief and reality can lead to misunderstandings, conflicts, and misinterpretations of the world. It is important to recognize and critically evaluate our beliefs to strive for a more accurate understanding of reality.

The intersection of these two presents an interesting phenomenon. This phenomenon occurs when the two elements overlap or interact with each other in a way that produces unexpected or unique results. It can lead to new insights, discoveries, or perspectives that may not have been apparent when considering each element separately. Exploring this intersection can provide valuable opportunities for learning, creativity, and problem-solving. By examining how these two elements intersect, we can gain a deeper understanding of their individual properties and how they influence each other.

Scripture:

Hebrews 11:1

"Now faith is the substance of things hoped for, the evidence of things not seen."

Devotional: Belief and Reality

The intersection of belief and reality is where our faith comes alive. Faith is not blind optimism; it's the bridge connecting the intangible promises of God with the tangible challenges of life. Hebrews 11:1 beautifully portrays faith as the "substance" and "evidence"—qualities that make hope feel real even when unseen.

Belief in God shapes how we perceive and respond to reality. It gives us the courage to face uncertainty, the wisdom to act in love, and the endurance to keep going. Reality doesn't always reflect the fullness of God's promises immediately, but faith assures us that His truths are at work behind the scenes.

Every act of kindness, every prayer offered, every choice to trust in challenging times—these moments of belief create ripples that shape reality. As we live by faith, we bring heavenly principles into earthly realms, weaving God's kingdom into our daily lives.

Prayer:

Heavenly Father,

Thank You for the gift of faith that connects us to Your promises. Help us walk boldly where belief and reality meet, trusting that You are faithful even when outcomes are unseen. Let our lives reflect Your truth, shaping our world with Your love and grace. Strengthen us to live out our faith in both the extraordinary and the mundane. In Jesus' name, Amen.

Reflective Questions:

1. How does your faith shape the way you interpret the challenges in your life?

2. Could you recall when your belief in God changed the course of your reality?

3. What steps can you take this week to align your actions with your faith, allowing belief to influence your daily reality?

18

Bloom Where Planted

"The Soil of Purpose"

Charles E. Cravey

In soil that's foreign, dry, or deep,

Our roots grow strong, though trials seep.

For where we're placed, by His design,

Is ground prepared for fruit divine.

The bloom may falter, petals may fade,

Yet beauty thrives where grace is laid.

Each thorn, each drought, each stormy hour,

Draws life anew to the budding flower.

Grow where planted, rise and spread,

Drink the rain where hope is fed.

Your season waits, your harvest near,

For God sustains the bloom sincere.

Though winds may howl and shadows fall,

His voice resounds above it all.

His gentle hand, unseen yet true,

Nourishes hearts with heavenly dew.

Among the rocks and barren plains,

Life finds a way through aching strains.

A lesson blooms in every place,

Of strength refined by saving grace.

The Gardener tends with loving care,

Each leaf, each stem, beyond compare.

He cultivates the soul to grow,

Through hidden paths we cannot know.

So bloom, dear soul, with roots held tight,

In present soil, bathed in His light.

For every struggle, every tear,

Is met with love that draws us near.

Wherever planted, His plan is wise,

Through humble soil, faith will arise.

The flower blooms, resilient, free,

A witness of His sovereignty.

Early in my ministry, I faced a challenging situation that often left me feeling discouraged. My assignment was to serve four churches on a charge, requiring me to preach at each church every Sunday. The schedule was demanding, with services scheduled at 9 am, 11 am, 3 pm, and 7 pm. This rigorous routine made it difficult to maintain the same level of enthusiasm and energy for each service as I navigated the unique dynamics and congregations of each church. Despite the challenges, I remained committed to delivering meaningful sermons and supporting the spiritual needs of each community.

Meeting with my district superintendent was a pivotal moment for me. I poured out my frustrations and concerns, seeking guidance and support. In response, he gave me a timeless piece of wisdom: "Bloom where you are planted." It reminded me to focus on making the best of my current situation, to grow and thrive regardless of the challenges I faced. The encouragement and insight I received during that meeting had a lasting impact on my perspective and approach to overcoming obstacles in both my personal and professional life.

Fifty years have passed since that pivotal moment shaped my faith and ministry journey. Despite facing challenges that could have led me away from the path, the guidance of a supportive superintendent kept me on course. Today, I continue to flourish and develop my spiritual calling, finding new ways to serve and grow daily. This transformative experience taught me the importance of seeking fresh perspectives and approaches to break free from stagnation and enhance productivity, compassion, and kindness towards others.

By embracing change and adopting a mindset of continuous improvement, I discovered a newfound capacity to bring about positive transformation in both my ministry and personal growth. As I navigated through the challenges and uncertainties of my journey, I learned the significance of self-reflection and self-improvement. By cultivating a mindset of openness and receptivity to innovative ideas, I could unlock hidden potential within myself and forge meaningful connections with others. Through acts of kindness, empathy, and genuine care, I witnessed the profound impact that small gestures can have on individuals and communities alike. Each day became an opportunity to learn, grow, and contribute to the betterment of those around me.

My journey of faith and ministry serves as a testament to the transformative power of perseverance, guidance, and personal growth. By embracing change, seeking new perspectives, and nurturing a spirit of kindness and compassion, we can overcome stagnation and unlock our true potential. I encourage you to reflect on your own journey, identify areas for improvement, and embark on a path of continuous learning and growth. The results of your efforts may surprise and inspire you, leading to a life filled with purpose, fulfillment, and positive impact.

Scripture:

Galatians 6:9

"And let us not be weary in well doing: for in due season we shall reap, if we faint not."

Devotional: "Bloom Where Planted"

"Bloom where planted" is a call to embrace and thrive in the circumstances God has entrusted to us. We may feel misplaced or wish for different surroundings, thinking that growth is only possible in ideal conditions.

But God's plans often stretch beyond our understanding, using the soil beneath us—whatever its quality—to nurture and grow us.

Galatians 6:9 assures us that perseverance in doing well, even in tough seasons, will lead to a harvest in God's perfect timing. Our task is not to pick the perfect ground but to trust His wisdom and grace in the place we are. Whether you're navigating challenges, embracing new opportunities, or seeking purpose in the mundane, remember that God's hand is at work, cultivating beauty and fruit in your life.

Prayer:

Dear Lord,

Thank You for placing us in the exact circumstances where Your purpose can unfold. Help us trust in Your timing and grace, allowing us to grow and thrive in every season. Teach us to embrace the soil beneath us and see it as part of Your divine plan. May we bloom where we are, shining Your light and bearing fruit that glorifies You. In Jesus' name, Amen.

Reflective Questions:

1. How do you perceive the circumstances in which you've been "planted"? Do you see opportunities for growth or feel resistant to them?

2. Could you recall a time when God helped you thrive in an unexpected or challenging environment?

3. What can you do today to embrace your current situation and trust God to guide your growth?

19

"I Can't Do This on My Own!"

"Held in His Hands"

Charles E. Cravey

When burdens press, too much to bear,
And shadows linger, everywhere,
My feeble strength begins to wane,
I call to Him through tears of pain.

Alone, the path seems dark and steep,
The hills too high, the valleys deep.
But in my weakness, love responds,
A Savior near, His grace beyond.

He whispers gently, "Lean on Me,
Through every trial, I'll set you free."
The weight I carry, His hands enfold,
A truth so constant, a love untold.

Not by my strength, nor by my might,
But by His Spirit, my soul takes flight.
In Him, I find the courage to stand,
To walk the road, held by His hand.

Mary found herself overwhelmed, juggling the responsibilities of work, family, and an unexpected financial hardship. She prided herself on being independent, often believing she had to carry her burdens alone. But as the stress mounted, so did her exhaustion, and she felt utterly defeated.

One evening, she broke down and confessed to God in prayer, "Lord, I can't do this alone anymore. I need you." At that moment, she felt a surprising peace—not because her circumstances changed right away, but because she realized she didn't have to bear the weight alone. She leaned into her faith, trusting that God's grace was sufficient, as Paul writes in 2 Corinthians 12:9.

Mary also reached out to a trusted friend from her church community, something she had hesitated to do before. She discovered her friend had walked a similar path and offered encouragement, practical help, and consistent prayers. Through God's guidance and the loving support of others, Mary slowly found solutions and strength she never thought possible.

The lesson Mary learned was this: admitting weakness and relying on God and others isn't failure—it's faith in action. We acknowledge our created purpose is connection—with God and the people He places in our lives to share burdens.

Scripture:

2 Corinthians 12:9

"My grace is sufficient for thee: for my strength is made perfect in weakness."

Devotional: "I Can't Do This Alone!"

Admitting "I can't do this alone" is not a sign of failure—it's an acknowledgment of our need for God's grace and strength. As humans, we often try to rely on our own abilities, striving to overcome challenges through sheer determination. But God calls us to lean on Him, reminding us that His grace is sufficient, especially in our moments of weakness.

In *2 Corinthians 12:9*, Paul shares how God's power is made perfect in our limitations. It's in those vulnerable places where we feel stretched thin, uncertain, and incapable that His strength shines brightest. God does not intend for us to face life's difficulties alone. God equips us with His presence and surrounds us with people to encourage and support us. Together, with Him and others, we can face what seems impossible.

Prayer:

Dear Lord,
In humility, we seek Your guidance, acknowledging our need for Your support in life's journey. We thank You for Your sustaining grace and Your strength in our weakness. Help us completely trust You and the people You've put in our lives. Grant us the strength to walk in Your power, aware that You sustain us through every trial.

In Jesus' name, Amen.

Reflective Questions:

1. What areas of your life feel overwhelming right now? Have you sought God's strength in these situations?

2. Who has God placed in your life to walk alongside you during difficult seasons? How can you lean into their support?

3. What steps can you take this week to release your burdens to God and trust His sufficiency?

20

A SEASON OF WAITING

"In the Stillness, He Works"

Charles E. Cravey

In muted moments, time stands still.

A season shaped by sovereign will.

The questions linger, the heart grows weak,

Yet in the waiting, it's Him we seek.

The seed lies dormant beneath the ground,

Awaiting sun and rain profound.

Though unseen, His hands prepare,

Each tender shoot with loving care.

Patience grows where hope resides,

Faith takes root; our God provides.

Through silence deep, His whisper guides,

In every pause, His grace abides.

As eagles rise through skies untamed,

We'll soar renewed, by strength reclaimed.

The season ends, His work complete.

Our souls refined for joys to meet.

I have always had a problem with patience, or rather, it has had a problem with me! The military uses the saying "Hurry up and wait" in basic training. This constant cycle can frustrate individuals like me who struggle with patience. The military's emphasis on urgency and readiness can exacerbate these struggles, but it also teaches valuable lessons in discipline and adaptability. Overall, the military's "hurry up and wait" mentality has been both a challenge and a learning experience for me in managing my patience. I realize that all of us will go through "seasons of waiting" in our lives. Those are the times that God is trying to speak to our will.

Starting his own business had always been Leonard's dream. Saving every penny, he dedicated himself to his business plan. He felt the time was right to apply for loans to realize his dream. The rejection of each application surprised him. Frustration washed over him as he questioned his pursuit of his dream.

Leonard offered a fervent prayer, seeking divine clarity and guidance. A seemingly endless period of waiting for an open door, guidance, and hope trapped him. Months passed, his weariness grew, yet Isaiah 40:31 offered comfort, its promise of renewed strength sustaining him.

During this time, Leonard spent the waiting season improving his skills and strengthening his faith. He built relationships with mentors, broadened his network, and gained insights from others' experiences. Despite slow progress, he found small encouraging signs: a mentor's kindness, a chance to shadow a business owner, and moments of prayerful peace.

Let us learn the art of waiting. We may be surprised by what we learn along the way!

Scripture:

Isaiah 40:31

"But they that wait upon the LORD shall renew their strength; they shall mount up with wings as eagles; they shall run, and not be weary; and they shall walk, and not faint."

Devotional: Waiting on God

Waiting often feels like a wilderness—a time of uncertainty, longing, and questions without answers. Yet, Isaiah 40:31 reminds us of the strength that comes from waiting on the Lord. Waiting is not a passive act; it's an active trust in His timing, wisdom, and plan.

In "seasons of waiting," God is at work within us, cultivating perseverance, refining our character, and deepening our faith. Just as a seed must stay in the soil until the right moment to sprout, we grow beneath the surface, unseen but deeply significant. It's through the waiting that we learn to rely on God's promises, not our own understanding.

Remember, God's delays are not denials. The season of waiting is purposeful, preparing us for the blessings to come. Trust Him in the stillness, for He is faithful to bring growth and renewal.

Prayer:

Dear Lord,

I thank You for the seasons of waiting that shape and refine us. Although patience is difficult, we have faith in your perfect timing and loving plan. As we wait on You, renew our strength, and help us accept the growth You're orchestrating in our lives. In Your presence, may we find peace, and in Your promises, assurance.

In Jesus' name, Amen.

Reflective Questions:

1. What feelings do you experience while waiting, and what strategies do you use to manage them?

2. Reflecting on a past season of waiting, how did God prepare you?

3. What does actively trusting God look like while you're waiting for something to happen?

21

SACRAMENTS OF FAITH

Sacraments of Faith

Charles E. Cravey

Blessed waters cleanse the soul,

Bread and wine make the faithful whole.

Sacred rites, a holy embrace,

Tokens of God's infinite grace.

In water, spirit, and sacred vow,

Heaven meets earth in the here and now.

Through sacraments, His love is shown,

A covenant made, a grace we've known.

Beneath the waters, calm and deep,

A promise made, a covenant to keep.

Baptism's grace, a soul reborn,

Like morning light at the break of dawn.

Bread is broken, the wine is poured,

Remembrance of Christ, our risen Lord.

His body given, His blood out-poured,

Our sins forgiven; love restored.

In sacred rites, God's presence stays,

A guiding light through all our days.

Symbols speak where words may fail,

Of mercy vast, of love unveiled.

Through the sacraments, heaven draws near,

God whispers hope that hearts may hear.

Faith's embrace in each holy sign,

His grace eternal, love divine.

These sacred moments call us higher,

To live in truth and to inspire.

A life of service, a heart made new,

Reflecting Christ in all we do.

Throughout my 53 years of ministry, I have had the privilege of administering Holy Communion in various settings, including youth camping trips. I have always approached this sacred duty and responsibility with the utmost reverence and fear of God. Whether in a traditional church setting or amidst the serenity of nature during a camping trip, I have always approached this practice with deep respect and solemnity. The act of serving the body and blood of Christ to the faithful is a humbling experience that requires careful preparation and a heart filled with devotion. In all my years of ministry, the administration of Holy Communion has been a cornerstone of my spiritual journey. I am grateful for the opportunities I have had to partake in this sacred ritual and am committed to continuing to carry out this duty with the same level of reverence and fear of God that has guided me throughout my ministry.

Once, while in Venezuela, I served communion to an indigenous tribe along the Apure River. An American missionary had converted them to Christianity, and it was deeply moving to celebrate communion with them in the Amazon. Each person took this act of communion with God seriously. There was a holy awe about the moments spent with them I shall never forget.

The next time you receive Holy Communion in your church setting, remember that tribe and be thankful. It is the body and blood of Jesus poured out and broken for YOU!

Scripture:

I Corinthians 11:26

"For as often as ye eat this bread, and drink this cup, ye do shew the Lord's death till he come."

Devotional: The Holy Sacraments

Christ instituted sacraments, outward signs signifying inward grace. These acts show worship and devotion, symbolizing the covenant between God and His people. Baptism, communion, and other holy ceremonies remind us of God's promises and His constant presence.

Christ's cleansing and uniting with us in baptism symbolizes the washing away of sin and the gift of new life. The Lord's Supper, or Communion, invites us to remember Christ's sacrifice—His body broken and His blood shed for us. Each sacrament is not only a ritual but also a living expression of faith and grace.

Let's reflect on the immense importance of these sacred rites as we celebrate them. We are called to live with renewed purpose, trust in God's promises, and share His grace with the world. These sacred acts remind us that faith is not a solitary journey, but one deeply connected to the body of Christ, His church, and His eternal love.

Prayer:

O Lord our God,

For the holy sacraments, signs, and seals of Your grace, we give thanks. Help us consume them reverently and gratefully, acknowledging your boundless love and mercy. May these holy rituals refresh our souls and bolster our belief, leading us nearer to God. We pray in the name of Jesus Christ, our Savior. Amen.

Reflective Questions:

1. How do the sacraments deepen your understanding of God's grace and love?

2. What personal significance does baptism or communion hold for you?

3. How can you live out the meaning of the sacraments in your daily walk of faith?

4. In what ways can you share the significance of the sacraments with others in your community?

22

THIS IS THE TIME

"This is the Time!"

Charles E. Cravey

This is the time, the moment, divine,

The clock is racing; the stars align.

Tomorrow fades, the call is clear,

Salvation beckons the Savior near.

No day but today, no chance but now.

Before Him in awe, every knee must bow.

This is the hour to turn and believe,

To find the grace hearts long to receive.

For fleeting are days, as shadows fade,

Life's fragile thread, in eternity, laid.

The door is open; the path is straight,

Come, weary soul, before it's too late.

Choose the light; His arms embrace.

Step into mercy, surrender to grace.

This is the time, no moment to lose,

God's love eternal—what will you choose?

As I was listening to an old Billy Joel song, "This is the Time," this morning, I couldn't help but think that the title would make a fitting introduction to an article about the unpredictability of life. We seldom realize the fragility of our existence and the unknown dangers that may lurk just around the corner.

Recently, a man of my age was out for a leisurely walk with his wife and dog, only to come home, sit in his favorite recliner, and suffer a sudden and fatal heart attack. This tragic event serves as a stark reminder that none of us know the day or hour when our time may come. Considering life's uncertainties, each moment becomes incredibly precious and fleeting. It's a poignant reminder to express our love and appreciation to those who matter most to us. It's a wake-up call to stop postponing our dreams and aspirations for a future that may never come. Instead, it's a time to seize the day and embrace the opportunities that lie before us. So, let's take this moment to cherish our loved ones, pursue our passions, and live each day to the fullest, for tomorrow is never guaranteed.

Scripture:

2 Corinthians 6:2

"(For he saith, I have heard thee in a time accepted, and in the day of salvation have I succoured thee: behold, now is the accepted time; behold, now is the day of salvation.)"

Each moment of our lives gives us a chance to connect more deeply with God. 2 Corinthians 6:2 highlights the urgency of salvation, reminding us that "now is the acceptable time."

The limitation of time makes each day a valuable gift. Like the ticking of a clock, our time on this earth is finite. God's boundless mercy, however, has opened salvation's door through Christ. He urges us to go through the open door. Believers find solace in their eternal security; those who haven't found their faith can start today.

Now is the moment to proclaim the good news, follow Christ courageously, and shower others with love. Daily, we're presented with opportunities: choose hope, peace, and faith instead of despair, turmoil, and fear. Will you heed His summons?

Prayer:

Gracious Lord,

We give thanks for Your mercy and the salvation You gave us through Christ. Let us seize this opportunity and answer God's pressing summons. Show us how to follow Your path, embracing each day as if it were our final one, and illuminating the world with Your light. Increase our faith and guide our response to Your love with hearts overflowing with gratitude and devotion.

In Jesus' name, Amen.

Reflective Questions:

1. How does the Scripture remind you of the importance of deciding for Christ today?

2. Is there someone in your life who needs to hear about salvation? How can you share it with them?

3. In what ways can you live each day with intentionality, reflecting the urgency of the gospel?

4. How can you better prepare your heart to respond to God's calling in this very moment?

23

LEAVE AN IMPRESSION

Leave an Impression

Charles E. Cravey

The paths we tread, the hearts we touch,

Our words, our deeds—they matter much.

In fleeting moments, life's quick dance,

We're called to love, to take the chance.

Through kindness shared and burdens borne,

We etch a mark, though time is worn.

A smile, a prayer, a hand to hold,

They whisper grace; they're treasures untold.

Leave an impression, bright and true,

Through actions pure love shining through.

The seeds we sow, the light we share,

Echo God's mercy everywhere.

For when our race comes to its end,

It's love that lingers; love transcends.

In Christ, we leave a legacy,

Of faith and hope for eternity.

In the heartwarming tale of "Forrest Gump," the protagonist poses a profound question to his mother one day: "Mama, what's my destiny?" This inquiry strikes a chord with audiences as it echoes a universal desire to understand one's purpose and place in the world. Just like Forrest, many of us grapple with the uncertainty of our destinies and seek clarity on the path ahead. The journey of self-discovery and seeking one's destiny is a theme that resonates deeply with viewers, reminding us of the importance of introspection and the quest for meaning in our lives.

"Forrest Gump" explores the idea of destiny through the life of its titular character, who navigates through various challenges and experiences while trying to make sense of his place in the world. Through Forrest's interactions with different people and his unique perspective on life, the film underscores the significance of embracing one's journey and finding purpose in the random events that shape our lives.

As the story unfolds, Forrest's question about his destiny becomes a poignant reflection of the human experience, prompting viewers to contemplate their own paths and the choices that define them. The film's exploration of destiny serves as a gentle reminder that, while life may be unpredictable and full of surprises, everyone has the power to shape their own narrative and create a meaningful existence. "Forrest Gump" invites audiences to ponder the timeless question of destiny and encourages them to embark on their own journey of self-discovery. Through Forrest's heartfelt quest for purpose and understanding, the film inspires viewers to embrace the unknown, trust in their inner voice, and believe in the possibility of shaping their destinies.

Scripture:

Matthew 5:16

"Let your light so shine before men, that they may see your good works, and glorify your Father which is in heaven."

Devotional: Leave an Impression

To leave an impression is to leave behind a trace of God's love in the lives of others. Matthew 5:16 calls us to let our light shine before men so they may glorify our Heavenly Father. Each interaction, whether big or small, holds the potential to create ripples that extend far beyond what we can see.

Christ left an everlasting impression on humanity through His love, sacrifice, and teachings. Likewise, we are called to reflect His light—to forgive, to comfort, to encourage. When we live lives of faith and compassion, we bear witness to God's transformative grace. Let us not underestimate the power of a kind word or a selfless act, for these are the echoes of Christ's love within us.

Prayer:

Father God,

Thank you for allowing us to be your instruments of faith and love, leaving a lasting impact. Instruct us in intentional living, mirroring Your light with each action and word. May our lives inspire others to find Your grace and may our acts of kindness create a legacy. Lead us each step of the way as we emulate Christ. Amen.

Reflective Questions:

1. What impression do you want to leave on the surrounding people?

2. How does Matthew 5:16 inspire you to live as a reflection of Christ's love?

3. Could you recall when someone's kindness left a deep impact on you?

4. How can you shine your light in your community or workplace today?

24

BLEMISHES OF LIFE

Blemishes

Charles E. Cravey

Scattered shadows, marks that stay,

Wounds from battles fought each day.

Blemishes of life, both seen and not.

Traces of trials, lessons they've brought.

Some marks we carry, etched so deep,

Memories awaken; they rarely sleep.

Yet in each scar, a story's told,

A thread of grace in sorrows of old.

For every stain, there lies a chance,

To rise anew, to take a stance.

In brokenness, God's light will gleam,

Redeeming pain, restoring the dream.

Blemishes speak of the path we've trod,

Yet in them shines the love of God.

A tapestry woven, imperfect yet bright,

Beauty reborn amid His light.

Blemishes are like scars in the sense that they can leave lasting marks on our skin. Blemishes refer to any imperfections or discolorations on the skin, such as acne, dark spots, or redness. These blemishes can be temporary or persistent, depending on numerous factors like skincare routine, genetics, and lifestyle choices. Similarly, scars are permanent marks left on the skin after a wound or injury has healed. Both blemishes and scars can affect our self-confidence and how we perceive ourselves. It is important to take care of our skin and seek treatment to minimize the appearance of blemishes and scars.

Scripture:

Psalm 147:3

"He healeth the broken in heart, and bindeth up their wounds."

Devotional: Life is Full of Blemishes

Imperfections—mistakes, setbacks, and sorrows that scar our spirits—mar life. We suffer some consequences because of our decisions, while the world's flaws force others upon us. While painful, these flaws are integral to our narrative. They serve as a reminder of our journey and progress.

However, God's love is beautiful because He overlooks our flaws. Psalm 147:3 assures us God heals the brokenhearted. Instead of representing defeat, our wounds and scars are proof of God's power and grace. God redeems and transforms the flawed, not discarding them. He heals our injuries and uses our imperfections to show His magnificence.

Through our imperfections, we find ourselves closer to Him, trusting in His strength instead of our own. Remember, on life's path, it's not our imperfections, but God's use of them in His plan that shapes who we are. Our flaws, through Christ, highlight the beauty of His perfect grace.

Prayer:

Lord of mercy and grace, before Thee we stand, burdened by life's imperfections—its burdens, scars, and wounds. We give thanks for Your boundless love, which finds beauty in our flaws. Mend our hearts, soothe our pain, and leverage our suffering to bring glory to Thee. Instill in us trust in Your salvation and inspire us to share our narratives as evidence of Your mercy. In Jesus' name, Amen.

Reflective Questions:

1. What blemishes or scars in your life have taught you the most about God's grace?

2. How does knowing that God heals and redeems bring comfort to your struggles?

3. Have you ever witnessed God using someone's imperfections to inspire or help others?

4. How can you embrace your own brokenness and allow God to transform it into something beautiful?

25

HAVE YOU EVER MOVED?

"Have You Ever Moved?"

Charles E. Cravey

Have you ever moved from a place once known,

Left behind the comforts you've outgrown?

The winding path, uncertain and new,

Where faith is tested and fears break through.

Each step, a story; each mile, a prayer.

In God's firm hands, your burdens He bears.

From valleys low to mountains steep,

He whispers promises His children keep.

Not all moves are made with feet alone.

The heart must shift where seeds are sown.

Growth requires a letting go,

To trust the One whose love we know.

So, move with faith, and leave the past,

For God's provision will hold you fast.

He leads you forward, step by step.

A life of purpose, divinely kept.

As an itinerant minister for fifty-three years, I have traversed various locations, often moving every four years. While there were a few instances where my wife, Renee, and I stayed put for five or six years, we were all too familiar with the transient nature of the preacher's life. Upon ordination, we solemnly vowed to "go where sent" with no hint of complaint. This commitment has led us on a journey filled with diverse experiences and challenges, shaping our ministry and deepening our faith along the way.

Imagine having to uproot your life every four years, disrupting your family. This is a reality for many pastors who are constantly on the move in service to the kingdom of God. Many consider this challenging and nomadic lifestyle necessary to revitalize churches that have become stagnant, introducing innovative ideas and growth. One of the primary reasons for pastors frequently moving is to breathe new life into churches that may have become stale and unmoving. A new pastor brings fresh perspectives, ideas, and energy, which can revitalize a congregation and lead to spiritual growth.

However, this constant turnover can also disrupt the stability and continuity of a church community, causing some members to feel unsettled and disconnected. Despite the challenges, many pastors see moving as a necessary sacrifice for the greater good of the church and its mission. They embrace the opportunity to serve different communities, learn from diverse experiences, and expand their spiritual horizons.

By being on the move, pastors can reach a wider audience and impact more lives with the message of God's love and grace. The life of a pastor on the move is a complex and challenging journey filled with both opportunities and hardships. Although uprooting oneself and starting anew may be difficult, many pastors see it as a crucial part of their calling to serve God's kingdom. By embracing change and uncertainty, pastors can bring about transformation and growth in churches that need revitalization. So, are you ready to join the ranks of those who are on the move for the sake of the gospel?

Scripture:

Matthew 4:19

"And he said unto them, follow me, and I will make you fishers of men."

Devotional: Have You Ever Moved?

Moving, be it physically, metaphorically, or spiritually, is always challenging. This requires venturing beyond the familiar into uncharted territory. But God frequently calls us to progress—to mature, trust, and follow Him wherever He guides.

In Matthew 4:19, Jesus asked His disciples to forsake their nets, their jobs, and their security to follow Him. This involved not only physical movement but spiritual movement, too. Their future was uncertain yet filled with eternal purpose.

Sometimes, God prompts us to act in our personal lives. We need a relocation, career change, or a change of heart—a transition from fear, resentment, and doubt to faith, forgiveness, and trust. Every action brings us closer to God and helps us fulfill His plan.

Have you ever sensed God prompting you to move? During life's transitions, His presence anchors us. He pledges to navigate us through uncertainty, meet our needs, and bring us to a place of growth and tranquility.

Prayer:

God, we're grateful for your unfailing guidance, especially during times of change and doubt. As we move forward in faith, teach us to place our complete trust in Thee. Let's shed our burdens and accept God's plan for our lives. Let our hearts be open, our spirits steadfast, as we follow Thee, trusting Thy presence to be with us always and everywhere. Amen, invoking the name of Jesus.

Reflective Questions:

1. Have you ever experienced a move—physically, emotionally, or spiritually—that challenged your faith?

2. What does it mean to you to "follow" God, even into the unknown?

3. How can you trust God more fully in moments of transition?

4. Is there something God might be calling you to leave behind in order to grow closer to Him?

26

"First Responders"

———◆———

"First Responders"

Charles E. Cravey

In life's chaos and the strife,

They bring hope; they save lives.

Hands steady, hearts brave,

First responders, lives they save.

Silent heroes, night and day,

Answering the call, come what may.

In darkness or daylight's radiant glow,

To perilous places, they steadfastly go.

With hands that heal, with hearts that care,

First responders answer every prayer.

Through raging fires, through crashing waves,

They press on boldly, and countless save.

Their courage shines where fears reside,

God's unseen hand is their constant guide.

I have witnessed the incredible dedication and bravery of our first responders during life-threatening situations. These selfless individuals are always ready to put their own lives on the line to help those in desperate need. We owe a debt of gratitude to these unsung heroes who work tirelessly around the clock to keep our communities safe.

One incident that stands out in my memory is when a house fire broke out in the neighborhood of one of my parishioners. The first responders' swift and heroic actions rescued a mother and her two children just in time. Their unwavering commitment to serving others in times of crisis is truly commendable. Let us never forget the sacrifices made by these brave men and women who embody the spirit of courage and compassion.

Scripture:

John 15:13

"Greater love hath no man than this, that a man lay down his life for his friends."

Devotional: "First Responders"

In times of crisis, first responders are often the first to step into the gap, offering aid, comfort, and hope. Their bravery reminds us of Christ's ultimate sacrifice—laying down His life for all of humanity. The Bible tells us in John 15:13 that there is no greater love than to give one's life for another. This scripture echoes through the actions of those who risk their lives daily to protect and serve.

Yet, even as these heroes go about their work doggedly, they carry immense burdens. They witness pain, sorrow, and despair. In these moments, they reflect a small portion of Christ's role as the ultimate healer and redeemer. Let us also remember that we are called to be responders in our faith—not necessarily in danger, but in daily acts of kindness, forgiveness, and love. How might we mirror such courage and selflessness in our own spiritual walk?

Prayer:

Lord God Almighty,

We offer our sincerest gratitude to all the first responders who so bravely and selflessly dedicate their lives to saving the lives of others. As they confront hardships that would crush most, we humbly beseech Thee, O Lord, to bestow upon them Thy divine protection and unwavering strength. May they find peace, resilience, and unwavering hope to help them through any hardships they may face. O Lord, we humbly beseech Thee to guide and instruct us in emulating the selfless example set by those who have served before us, that we too may serve others in Thy name with unwavering devotion and humility. May all that we do and say bring glory and honor to Thee, both now and forevermore. Amen.

Reflective Questions:

1. How does the sacrifice of first responders remind you of Christ's sacrifice on the cross?

2. In what ways can you show courage and selflessness in your faith

journey?

3. Is there someone in your life who is a first responder? How might you support or encourage them today?

4. What steps can you take to be a "spiritual first responder," offering hope and light in the lives of others?

27

Soup Kitchen Stories

Soup Kitchen Stories

Charles E. Cravey

In a humble hall with tables spread,

Hands serve love, and hearts are fed.

Stories shared beneath the glow,

Of simple meals where grace does flow.

The rich, the poor, the broken, the healed,

In the warmth of service, hearts are revealed.

Each ladle lifted, each smile bestowed,

God's kindness blooms where love is sowed.

Lives entwine in the muted grace.

Souls redeemed in this sacred space.

Here, Christ's example shines so bright,

Feeding the hungry, offering light.

For the least of these, we dare to care,

Echoing mercy, a gift so rare.

Soup kitchen stories, a glimpse divine,

Of God's great love in humble design.

Over the years, I've encountered many people coping with heartbreak at the soup kitchens our church has supported. Those with broken spirits search for a warm meal and human connection. These are among the most significant community services a church can provide. However, it requires many dedicated individuals to embody Christ's compassion and service to those beyond our community.

I used to play my guitar and sing for the homeless and destitute at a large soup kitchen in Macon, Georgia, once a month during lunchtime. My biggest reward from those events was the friendships I formed with people outside the usual church circles. One time, I encountered a homeless man from Chicago sleeping under a bridge. Heartbreak filled his story. After 32 years, he lost his job and, being older and unskilled, struggled to find alternative employment. Abandoned by his wife, he journeyed with his two children, traveling from town to town, crossing countless bridges. I recall praying with him that day, wishing him well, and I still wonder what happened to him. The soup kitchen holds stories of real lives, genuine struggles, and broken hearts. I remember hearing, "But for the grace of God, there go you and I," a saying that is quite thought-provoking.

Scripture:

Matthew 25:35

"For I was an hungred, and ye gave me meat: I was thirsty, and ye gave me drink: I was a stranger, and ye took me in."

Devotional: Soup Kitchen Stories

The soup kitchen provides more than just sustenance. Matthew 25:35 reminds us that when we serve the hungry, the thirsty, and the stranger, we are serving Christ Himself.

Each meal served shows compassion and obedience to God. It's more than about feeding people. It's about listening to the stories of those who feel forgotten, sharing smiles that spark hope, and showing that someone cares.

Soup kitchens embody God's kingdom on Earth. They bring to mind Christ's humility and His charge to help the most vulnerable.

Prayer:

Loving Father, we thank you for the places of grace where people touch lives and share hope. May blessings be upon those who serve, those with compassionate hearts, and those humble souls in need. Help us recognize Christ in all people and serve them with love and compassion. Guide us to fulfill Your purpose, affecting the lives of others. Amen, in the name of Jesus.

Reflective Questions:

1. How do soup kitchens embody the teachings of Christ in Matthew 25:35?

2. Have you ever taken part in serving others in need? What did you

learn from the experience?

3. How can you apply the spirit of compassion and service from soup kitchens to your daily life?

4. What stories of hope and transformation inspire you to serve others with humility?

—◁◇◇▷—

28

METAPHORICAL ALTAR CALL

Metaphorical Altar Call

Charles E. Cravey

The altar stands, though not of stone.

It's built in hearts, in lives alone.

A sacred call, a whispered plea,

Come now, my child, draw near to Me.

No church walls bound, no pulpit's cry,

This altar stretches to the sky.

It's in the fields, it's on the street,

In broken places where hearts meet.

No steps to climb, no hands to raise,

Just simple faith and love ablaze.

The call goes out in every land,

Come, take the Savior's outstretched hand.

Lay down your burdens, your sin, your shame,

The One who knows you calls your name.

A metaphor, but real and true,

An altar call for me and you.

This sacred moment, this holy space,

Where mercy meets us face to face.

The altar calls, it always stands,

Where hearts are open, where love commands.

I met Jesus one night at a darkened church altar in my hometown. It was a transformative time for me as I prayed together with two friends. We were the only ones there, save the Holy Spirit. That night, God's grace and mercy filled my heart in a wonderful way. I was only eighteen, but now my horizons would expand to a wonderful lifetime of ministry to God's people from all levels of society. From the jungles of Guyana to the plains of Spain, God has used me to impart his word and grace to all people. What a beginning that night turned out to be.

Have you made that metaphorical altar call? Your altar can be anywhere—in a car, at home, with a friend, etc. There are unseen altars everywhere, beckoning us to draw near and to receive God's abundance.

Scripture:

Matthew 11:28

"Come unto me, all ye that labour and are heavy laden, and I will give you rest."

Devotional: Metaphorical Altar Call

The altar call doesn't have to happen in a church sanctuary. It's not confined to a set moment in a worship service. Instead, the altar call is a metaphor for God's constant invitation to draw near to Him, wherever we are. Matthew 11:28 reminds us that Christ calls out to the weary, the burdened, and the broken—and He promises rest.

Moments tug at our hearts, calling us to lay our burdens at the feet of Christ. We do not build these "altars" of wood or stone, but of humility and faith. Whether it's in the quiet of our rooms, amid chaos, or in a whispered prayer during a tough moment, we can respond to the call.

The beauty of the altar call is its accessibility. God meets us where we are, offering grace and renewal. And just as Christ invites us to come, we, too, can extend this call to others. Through kindness, love, and prayer, we can show others the way to His open arms.

Prayer:

Gracious Lord, we are thankful for your call that finds us, wherever we may be. Your compassion is limitless, and Your affection draws us close. Help us approach You with open hearts, prepared to surrender our burdens and find Your peace. Guide us to recognize and respond to Your call each day and enable us to bring others to Your saving grace. Let it be so, in the name of Jesus.

Reflective Questions:

1. How does the idea of a "metaphorical altar call" remind you of God's constant invitation?

2. Where in your daily life do you feel called to draw closer to Christ?

3. What burdens might you need to surrender at this altar today?

4. How can you reflect God's invitation and love to someone who needs it?

29

"Bright, SunShiny Day!"

"Bright, SunShiny Day"

Charles E. Cravey

The skies declare a radiant glow,

A day of promise, grace to show.

The clouds have parted, shadows fade,

Bright, sunshiny day, in hope arrayed.

Each beam a whisper, a soft embrace,

A glimpse of God's unending grace.

The flowers bloom, the birds take flight,

A symphony of pure delight.

Oh, wondrous day of light so clear,

A reminder that God is ever near.

Through storms we've weathered, tears we've cried,

His faithfulness stands, a steady guide.

Let joy spring forth, let faith arise.

As sunlight dances in endless skies.

This bright, sunshiny day, a gift anew,

A canvas painted with mercy's hue.

So, lift your eyes, give thanks and sing,

For every bright day, His blessings bring.

Let love and hope light the way,

On this bright, sunshiny day!

I remember a song from "Brothers of the Heart" entitled "I Can See Clearly Now" that really touched me. In the very first verse, the words state, "Gone are the dark clouds that had me blind. It's gonna be a bright, bright, sunshiny day." This line conveys a wonderful thought of all our dark clouds disappearing, symbolizing hope and positivity. The song's uplifting message resonates with listeners, reminding them that brighter days are ahead despite challenging times. The lyrics of "Bright, Sunshiny Day" inspire a sense of optimism and serve as a source of comfort during difficult moments.

In our journey through life, we inevitably encounter dark clouds that overshadow our days and dampen our spirits. These clouds represent the challenges, struggles, and uncertainties that we face. However, amidst the darkness, there is a source of light and hope that shines through - God's grace. This divine grace has the power to lift us out of despair, guiding us towards a path of healing, renewal, and spiritual growth.

God's grace serves as a beacon of light, piercing through the clouds of adversity and illuminating our hearts with love and compassion. It is through this grace that we can see beyond our immediate circumstances and gain a deeper understanding of the greater purpose at play in our lives. Just as the sun breaks through the clouds after a storm, God's grace brings warmth and rejuvenation to our weary souls.

In moments of darkness and despair, it is essential to remember that God's grace is ever-present, offering us solace and strength to endure life's challenges. By embracing this grace, we can find light behind the clouds and experience the transformative power of divine love in our lives. Let us open our hearts to God's grace and allow it to lead us towards a brighter tomorrow, filled with hope, faith, and unwavering trust in His plan for us.

Scripture:

Psalm 118:24

"This is the day which the LORD hath made; we will rejoice and be glad in it."

Devotional: "Bright, Sunshiny Day!"

Each radiant, sunny day displays God's goodness and calls us to celebrate His creation. Psalm 118:24 reminds us to view each day as a divine gift, filled with joy and hope. Although life includes storms and trials, the sunlight breaking through reminds us that God's mercies are new each morning.

Today's brightness reflects the light of Christ within us. Like the sun banishing darkness, His presence banishes fear, sorrow, and doubt. On days like these, let's appreciate the many blessings in our lives, both big and small, and thank Him for His unwavering faithfulness.

Even with cloudy skies, remember the sun's still shining. Similarly, God's love and promises are unwavering, regardless of the situation. May the joy of this radiant day fill our hearts and brighten the lives of those we encounter, as we reflect His light to the world.

Prayer:

We thank you, Father, for this radiant sunny day, a testament to Your love and faithfulness. Guide us to celebrate each moment, notice Your blessings everywhere, and shine Your light on others. Let the happiness of today stay with us, for God is always with us. Amen, in the name of Jesus.

Reflective Questions:

1. How does Psalm 118:24 encourage you to find joy and gratitude in your day?

2. What are some "bright sunshiny" moments in your life that remind you of God's goodness?

3. How can you reflect the light of Christ in the lives of others today?

4. Even in challenging times, how do you hold on to the truth of God's unchanging love?

30

ANCHORS THAT HOLD

Anchors that Hold

Charles E. Cravey

When stormy seas begin to rise,

And fear clouds over hopeful skies,

When winds may howl and waters cold,

We cling to anchors strong and bold.

Not made of iron, nor forged by men,

These anchors rest in God's hand.

Faith unmoved, though tempests roar,

A steady hope forevermore.

An anchor holds, though eyes may weep,

In trials vast, its grip runs deep.

God's promises, they will not wane,

A firm foundation through the strain.

When doubts assail, and paths seem dim,

Our anchor steadies, rooted in Him.

Through every storm, through broken night,

God is the anchor, our guiding light.

So, fear not storms, nor waves untamed,

The Anchor holds in His great name.

Through troubled seas, His grace abounds,

In Christ alone, true hope is found.

A few years ago, I took my wife Renee on a Caribbean cruise. Eager for the adventure ahead, we set sail on the vast ocean, ready to explore new destinations and create unforgettable memories. However, the journey took an unexpected turn when Renee experienced severe seasickness, also known as vertigo, which made her cruise experience challenging.

Despite being prepared with patches behind her ear to ease the symptoms, Renee found little relief. She struggled with the constant feeling of the giant ocean liner moving beneath her feet, causing discomfort and unease throughout the trip.

In contrast, I felt none of the motion that Renee described, experiencing smooth sailing and enjoying the beauty of the open sea. Renee's battle with seasickness during our Caribbean cruise serves as a reminder of the unpredictable nature of travel and the importance of being prepared for unforeseen challenges. Despite the obstacles she faced, Renee's resilience and determination to make the most of the journey were truly inspiring, and our shared experience created a bond that strengthened our love for one another.

Scripture:

Hebrews 6:19

"Which hope we have as an anchor of the soul, both sure and stedfast, and which entereth into that within the veil."

Devotional: Anchors that Hold

An anchor serves a vital purpose—it holds a vessel steady amidst the storms. Hebrews 6:19 portrays hope as the anchor of our souls, secure and steadfast and grounded in God's promises. Unlike earthly anchors, God's anchor does not shift, falter, or break. It holds us fast, no matter the intensity of the storm.

Life often feels like turbulent waters. Trials, losses, and uncertainties can make us feel adrift, vulnerable to being swept away. Yet, through it all, God offers us an anchor—a firm foundation in His Word, His promises, and His eternal love. This anchor not only keeps us grounded but also gives us hope, enabling us to endure. Christ is the ultimate anchor. His sacrifice, resurrection, and unfailing grace secure our souls for eternity. When we tether ourselves to Him, the storm cannot isolate us.

Prayer:

Eternal Father, we are grateful for your steadying presence amidst life's storms. During tumultuous times, we pray to remain steadfast with Thee.

Fortify our faith and uplift our hearts with hope. Instill in us trust in Your pledges, understanding Your steadfastness and certainty. May your love comfort us grant security always. Amen, invoking the name of Jesus.

Reflective Questions:

1. What storms have you faced where God's presence acted as an anchor for your soul?

2. How does Hebrews 6:19 encourage you to hold on to hope during trials?

3. Are there areas in your life where you feel adrift? How can you anchor yourself more firmly in Christ?

4. How can you share the hope of Christ as an anchor with someone who is struggling?

31

"Forgive Them, Father"

"Forgive Them, Father"

Charles E. Cravey

Upon the hill, where shadows fell,

The Savior bore the weight of hell.

Through scorn and nails, His love declared,

"Forgive them, Father," His soul bared.

Their hearts were hard, their vision blind.

Yet mercy bloomed—a love so kind.

For each transgression, He forgave,

And through His blood, the lost He'd save.

Oh, human hearts, so frail and weak,

Hear now the words the Savior speaks.

Let hatred die, let love arise.

Forgive, as Christ, who reigns on high.

The cross's cry, His gift of grace,

Invites us all to seek His face.

"Forgiveness Like the Dawn"

The morning breaks, the night must yield,

The Savior prays, His wounds unsealed.

Upon the cross, where mercy flows,

"Forgive them, Father," grace bestows.

Their mockery, a cruel refrain,

Each lash, each nail, their hateful gain.

Yet in His voice, no wrath is borne.

A love so pure, it shames the scorn.

For every sin, His blood was shed,

For every wound, He bowed His head.

Forgiveness vast, as ocean wide,

In Him, the lost may yet abide.

Oh, weary soul, with burdens great,

Release the chains, release the hate.

Let Christ's example show the way

To love, to peace, a brighter day.

And when the dawn dispels the night,

His mercy shines, His truth, our light.

Forgiveness, not a fleeting flame,

But life's great gift, in Jesus' name.

The pain of rejection was the biggest pain to Jesus on that rugged cross of Calvary that Good Friday. His very disciples had denied having known him. That pain was worse than the nails being driven through his hands and feet. He had given them the three best years of his life, teaching and training them about a better way of life. It hurt, I'm sure, to have looked down upon those who had condemned him to death and yet express his forgiveness for them in this beautiful phrase: "Father, forgive them, for they know not what they do."

Often, we may feel rejected by the very ones we love. How we respond in those moments should exemplify the love and forgiveness of Christ without ridicule or anger. Our lives should be beacons of Christ, shining forth for all to see and witness.

Scripture:

Luke 23:34: "Then said Jesus, Father, forgive them; for they know not what they do. And they parted his raiment, and cast lots."

Devotional: "Father, Forgive Them"

When Jesus hung on the cross, enduring unimaginable agony, He chose to offer forgiveness instead of condemnation. His words, "Father, forgive them," were not spoken out of weakness but out of divine love and strength. In this moment, Jesus demonstrated the ultimate act of grace, pleading for those who mocked, scorned, and crucified Him.

Consider the depth of His mercy. If Christ could forgive such grievous offenses, can we not strive to forgive the smaller transgressions we face daily? Forgiveness is not about excusing wrongdoing but about freeing our hearts from the chains of resentment. It is an act of trust in God's justice and a step towards healing.

Let us follow the example of our Savior, learning to release bitterness and embrace the transformative power of forgiveness.

Prayer:

Heavenly Father, we come before You, humbled by the example of Your Son. In His suffering, He showed mercy; in His anguish, He chose grace. Teach us to forgive as He forgave, even when it feels impossible. Soften our hearts, Lord, and help us release any anger or bitterness we hold. Let us trust in Your justice and lean on Your strength as we strive to walk in love and mercy. May we reflect Christ's heart in all we do. Amen.

Reflective Questions:

1. Is there someone in your life you find difficult to forgive? What steps can you take to move toward forgiveness?

2. How does Jesus' example of forgiveness challenge or encourage you in your own relationships?

3. What does forgiveness mean to you personally, and how has it shaped your spiritual journey?

32

THE SPIRITUAL TOUCH

"The Spiritual Touch"

Charles E. Cravey

A gentle whisper, a healing hand,

A touch unseen yet deeply grand.

The Spirit moves, ignites the soul,

Revives the broken, makes us whole.

Through shadows dark, His presence stays.

Guiding hearts through an endless maze.

A sacred touch, both firm and mild,

Turns wayward paths to reconciled.

No walls can bar, no heart too cold,

His love persists; His grace unfolds.

Each touch divine, each moment true,

Reveals His strength, renews our view.

Throughout my life and ministry, I have been touched by Jesus' miraculous hand on numerous occasions. There have been sacred moments at the altar when a poor soul required God's strength and power to touch them and reaffirm their role as vital links in God's kingdom. Often through tears, I shared those precious moments with them and felt God move in miraculous ways.

I have felt God's presence at the bedside of a dying parishioner in those precious moments before they passed away. I could feel God's presence in a very tangible way through family members who had also witnessed their loved one's homegoing.

I know you have felt His presence before, and perhaps at other points in your life when you were not sure who touched you. It is truly a blessing to experience His strength, power, and comfort at times like these.

Scripture:

John 14:26

"But the Comforter, which is the Holy Ghost, whom the Father will send in my name, he shall teach you all things, and bring all things to your remembrance, whatsoever I have said unto you."

Devotional: "The Spiritual Touch"

"The Spiritual Touch" serves as a reminder that the Holy Spirit is present in our lives. His touch is often subtle but profoundly impactful, guiding, comforting, and transforming us. As believers, we can sense His presence in times of need, when peace breaks through chaos or clarity emerges from the fog of confusion.

The Holy Spirit is referred to as the Comforter, sent by the Father to live within and teach us. This touch is not only a sign of love, but also an ongoing invitation to lean into His presence, seek His guidance, and embrace His transformative power.

How often do you pause in your daily life to acknowledge the Spirit is presence? Let us cultivate a sense of His presence, believe in His wisdom, and open our hearts to His divine intervention.

Prayer:

Dear Heavenly Father,

Thank You for the Holy Spirit, the Comforter, who works miracles in our lives. Help us to be attentive to His presence and open to His guidance. May His touch heal our wounds, soothe our fears, and guide our paths. Teach us to seek Your Spirit in everything we do, and to believe in Your promise that You are always with us. May our lives be living proof of the transformative power of Your touch. Amen.

Reflective Questions:

1. Can you recall a moment when you felt the Holy Spirit's touch in your life? How did it affect you?

2. In what ways can you become more aware of the Spirit's presence daily?

3. How can you allow His touch to guide your decisions and actions?

33

Our Church's Sacred Call

A Beacon's Call

Charles E. Cravey

Upon the hill, the church bells chime.

Their echoes reach beyond the time.

A sacred call to far and near,

To bring the lost, to soothe the fear.

The hands of Christ, in service we,

To bind the broken and set them free.

Through every storm, His light will shine.

Our sacred call, His love divine.

We gather here, both weak and strong,

To find our place, to sing the song.

United hearts, in faith we stand,

To spread His word across the land.

No boundary set, no work too small,

For in His name, we give our all.

Our church, a vessel for His grace,

A beacon bright in every place.

O sacred call, we hear the sound,

In Christ alone, our lives are found.

Forevermore, we walk His way,

A mission clear, until that day.

My minister, Pastor Mark, spoke to us last Sunday about the church's sacred call to reach out to others, to love them in Jesus' name, and to be the church outside of the walls we worship in. His message was powerful and moving, providing the exact balm our church needed at the time. We have been in a transition period since the church split over a major issue, and we have been recovering from our losses. However, by God's grace, we are now growing and moving forward with a pastor who has a clear vision for the future and a heart as stimulating as a mountain stream. He has been a blessing to our church, leading us forward in faith.

We must all take seriously the church and God's sacred call to reach out to others and welcome them back into the church, to seek out the lost, and to minister to the needy. There is so much work to be done in our world today, and we are called to be change agents. See you at church this Sunday!

Scripture:

Mark 16:15

"And he said unto them, Go ye into all the world, and preach the gospel to every creature."

Devotional: "Our Church's Sacred Mission"

Our church's sacred call is based on Jesus' Great Commission, which directs us to spread His message and love throughout the world. This divine calling is not limited to the confines of a building but extends into our daily lives, encouraging us to be living examples of grace, compassion, and faith.

As members of Christ's body, we are called to be His hands and feet—to feed the hungry, console the bereaved, and lift the downtrodden. Every act of kindness, every prayer uttered, and every truth shared contributes to the fulfillment of this sacred mission.

Let us embrace our church's calling with joy and purpose, knowing that we are a part of something much bigger than ourselves. May we work together as one in Christ, allowing His Spirit to guide and His love to shine through us.

Prayer:

Dear Father, we thank You for calling us to be Your vessels of love and truth. Unite us as a church so that we can fulfill the sacred mission You have given us. Strengthen our hearts, motivate our actions, and lead us in Your ways. Help us reach out to those in need, proclaim Your gospel boldly, and shine Your light in a dark world. May our church be a shining example of Your grace, and may we honor You in all that we do. Amen.

Reflective Questions:

1. How can you personally contribute to your church's mission and sacred call?

2. Are there ways your church can better serve the community and spread the gospel?

3. What steps can you take to become more involved in fulfilling God's call through the church?

34

MAMA'S LONE ROSE

Mama's Rose

Charles E. Cravey

In Mama's yard, a rose once grew,

Its petals kissed by morning dew.

A lone bloom bright, its fragrance sweet,

Her gentle care made it complete.

But time moved on; the house now sold,

Her hands, once warm, no longer hold.

Yet in my heart, her love remains.

Through memories fond and fleeting pains.

I dug her rose, so frail yet strong,

A symbol of where you belong.

Transplanted now, it takes its place,

In my own garden, her embrace.

Each year it blooms—just one, no more.

A gift that knocks upon the door.

It whispers soft, "She's always near.

Her love's alive; no need to fear."

Mama's rose, a sacred tie,

That binds me to her when I sigh.

Though earthly farewells must impart,

Her bloom remains within my heart.

My mom died fifteen years ago. She was a huge fan of all things blooming. Our yard was always adorned with flowers, fruit trees, and her roses. She used to tell us kids that when she died, she wanted only one rose in her casket. She adored her roses and treated them with the care that a mother would give to her children.

When Mama died, before we sold the house, I dug up her favorite rose bush and planted it in my own yard next to my birdbath. It has remained there for the past fifteen years, producing only one rose each year. As I recall, it produced numerous buds and roses during her lifetime, but only one now. I suppose it is Mama's way of reminding me that she is still with me. But how does a child forget their mother?

Scripture:

Song of Solomon 2:1

"I am the rose of Sharon, and the lily of the valleys."

Devotional: "Just One Rose Will Do"

The lone rose from my mother's yard is more than a flower; it's a tangible reminder of love and connection. Just as this rose blooms once a year, so do the memories of Mama fill my heart with vibrant beauty. This bloom is a testament to the enduring bonds between a mother and her child—bonds not limited by time or place.

God often works through creation to remind us of His promises. The Bible speaks of the "rose of Sharon" as a symbol of beauty, love, and renewal. Mama's rose represents her love blooming in my life, a love that transcends the physical and whispers of eternity.

Each year, when her rose blooms, I will let it be a reminder of God's grace and the gift of my mother's enduring presence in my heart. I will cherish the bloom and cherish the memories, for they are eternal gifts from the Creator.

Prayer:

Dear Heavenly Father,

We thank You for the love and memories You grant us, especially through those who are no longer with us. Mama's lone rose is a beautiful reminder of Your grace and of a mother's eternal bond with her child. Bless me as I tend to this flower, and may each bloom be a whisper of her love and Your presence. Comfort us in moments of grief and fill our hearts with peace. In Jesus' name, Amen.

Reflective Questions:

1. How does my mother's lone rose remind you of God's spirit and love?

2. What lessons from this story inspire you today?

3. Does this story bring us closer to God's presence and comfort?

35

LAUNCH OUT INTO THE DEEP!

Launch Out!

Charles E. Cravey

The shoreline feels so safe, so sure.

Where waters calm and paths endure.

Yet whispers call from oceans wide,

"Launch out," they say, "let faith abide."

The shallow streams may soothe the soul.

But deeper waters make us whole.

For in the depths, His wonders reign,

Through unscaled heights and unseen plain.

Oh, trembling heart, let courage rise,

For He who calls, the seas He ties.

Though waves may roar, and winds may wail,

His voice will still, and His love prevails.

So, raise the sails, let anchors lift,

Step out in faith and embrace His gift.

For treasures lie where doubts recede,

Launch out into the deep—proceed.

In Luke 5:4, we find a beautiful and powerful command from Jesus to his disciples. The passage instructs them to "launch out into the deep." This command is not just about physical navigation but also carries deep spiritual significance. By urging his disciples to venture into the deep waters, Jesus is calling them to step out of their comfort zones, to trust in him completely, and to embrace the unknown with faith and courage.

Just as the disciples had to have faith in Jesus' words to cast their nets into the deep waters, we, too, are called to trust in God's guidance and take bold steps in our journey of faith. This passage serves as a reminder for us to go beyond the shallow waters of familiarity and safety and instead to venture into the depths of God's plan for us.

Where may the grace of God be calling you today?

Scripture:

Luke 5:4

"Now when he had left speaking, he said unto Simon, Launch out into the deep, and let down your nets for a draught."

Devotional: "Launch Out!"

Jesus' command to Simon Peter to "launch out into the deep" goes far beyond a simple fishing instruction; it is an invitation to trust Him fully. Though the disciples toiled all night without success, at Jesus' word, they cast their nets into the deep—and then they received an abundance of fish, more than they could manage.

It's natural to want to stay in the safety of the shallow waters, where life feels predictable and comfortable. However, Jesus calls us to step out of our comfort zones, to take risks in faith, and to trust in His provision and guidance. Launching out into the deep is not without its struggles, but it is in those depths that we experience the fullness of God's power and grace.

Let us answer His call today with courage, knowing that He is always in the boat with us, leading us to deeper faith and greater blessings.

Prayer:

Dear Lord, You invite us to step out in faith, leaving the safety of the shore, trusting You in life's deep waters. Empower us to release our fears and doubts, trusting in Your limitless power and provision. Bolster our faith, reminding us of Your constant guidance and provision in all circumstances. Grant us the courage to heed Your call and accept the gifts of our faith in You. Amen.

Reflective Questions:

1. What "deep waters" in your life might God be calling you to launch into?

2. How does this scripture challenge you to trust God more fully?

3. In what areas of your life do you need to step out of your comfort zone and embrace deeper faith?

36

Uncommitted

Uncommitted

Charles E. Cravey

The path divides, a choice unclear,

The call of truth, a voice sincere.

Yet footsteps falter, hearts delay,

Uncommitted, led astray.

One hand on faith, one in the world,

A fleeting sail, by tempests hurled.

The Master pleads, "Choose ye this day,"

Yet doubts and fears still hold their sway.

Oh, wavering soul, torn in two,

God's love awaits, His grace is true.

Forsake the drift, embrace the shore,

Commit your heart forevermore.

No half-measured vow, no fleeting flame,

But steadfast faith in Jesus' name.

For blessings flow where trust abides,

And in His will, the soul resides.

The concept of uncommitted conjures up a plethora of thoughts, sparking curiosity and contemplation. It evokes a sense of ambiguity and uncertainty, leaving room for interpretation and exploration. We can see the idea of being uncommitted in various aspects of life, such as relationships, career choices, and personal beliefs. It challenges traditional notions of commitment and highlights the fluidity of human experiences. By delving deeper into the concept of uncommitted, one can uncover a rich tapestry of emotions, perspectives, and possibilities. This document aims to explore the multifaceted nature of uncommitted and its implications on individuals and society.

In the realm of human experience, the uncommitted represent a diverse and multifaceted group that offers a unique perspective on life. By examining their thoughts, feelings, and potential choices, we can gain a deeper understanding of this often overlooked segment of society.

The uncommitted encompasses a wide range of individuals who may be hesitant to fully engage in various aspects of life. They may exhibit a sense of ambivalence or uncertainty towards making decisions, whether in relationships, career paths, or personal goals. This hesitancy can stem from a multitude of factors, such as fear of failure, lack of clarity, or a desire to explore different options before committing.

Despite their indecision, the uncommitted often possess a rich inner world filled with complex emotions and conflicting desires. They may oscillate between feelings of freedom and constraint, longing for stability, yet craving novelty and excitement. This internal struggle can lead to a constant state of flux, where the uncommitted navigate the delicate balance between security and risk.

The perspectives of the uncommitted offer a valuable lens through which to view the world. Their reluctance to conform to societal expectations or predefined norms allows them to challenge existing paradigms and question the status quo. By embracing uncertainty and ambiguity, the uncommitted open themselves up to a world of endless possibilities and potential discoveries.

In conclusion, the uncommitted represent a vibrant and dynamic segment of society that embodies the beauty of human complexity. By exploring their emotions, perspectives, and possibilities, we can gain a deeper appreciation for the richness and diversity of the human experience. Let us embrace the uncommitted, not as indecisive or passive individuals, but as courageous explorers of the unknown, charting their own path through the intricate tapestry of life.

Within the church's congregation, those who have yet to commit themselves, while having attended services for an extended period, represent a group of individuals who haven't made a formal decision to join the church or deepen their involvement within the church community. We must pay attention to them and what they say, for it is people like them who make up God's kingdom, and to ignore them would be a great disservice.

Scripture:

Revelation 3:16

"So then because thou art lukewarm, and neither cold nor hot, I will spue thee out of my mouth."

Devotional: The Uncommitted

A lack of commitment leads to indecision and spiritual stagnation. Revelation 3:16 cautions the Laodicean church against lukewarmness, neither hot nor cold. This stark imagery reminds us that God wants complete devotion, not divided loyalty.

Hesitation prevents us from experiencing the abundant life God intends for us. An uncommitted heart vacillates between faith and doubt, obedience, and ease. Despite this, God's boundless love persistently urges us to abandon neutrality and embrace Him fully.

Commitment demands sacrifice, courage, and trust. But it is through wholehearted dedication that we experience the depth of His promises, the joy of His presence, and the power of His Spirit working within us. Let us no longer linger in indecision but boldly commit ourselves to God, holding nothing back.

Prayer:

Heavenly Father, we ask for Your forgiveness for our wavering commitment, torn between worldly desires and Your divine will. We pray for the strength to surrender completely to You and dedicate our lives to Your glory. Guide us to trust Your plans and walk bravely in faith, free from doubt and fear. May we passionately devote our hearts to You, and may our lives show our unwavering devotion. Amen, we pray in the name of Jesus.

Reflective Questions:

1. Are there areas of your life where you feel uncommitted to God? What steps can you take to fully surrender those areas to Him?

2. How does being "lukewarm" affect your relationship with God and others?

3. What does wholehearted commitment to God look like in your daily walk of faith?

1.

37

The Unsung Heroes

"To Those Who Held Me Up"

Charles E. Cravey

To every hand that held me high,

To every heart that heard my cry,

To those who cheered when I was weak,

Who lent their strength when I'd not speak.

You've shaped my path; you've lit my way.

Your love has brightened every day.

Through trials faced, and joys embraced,

Thanks to you, my soul's been graced.

For kindness given, for time bestowed,

For lifting burdens from my load.

You are the hands, the hearts that bless,

Reflecting Christ's own tenderness.

So here I stand, in gratitude,

For all you've done, for all that's good.

May God reward and guard your care,

And keep you always in His share.

Countless souls have blessed me with their support throughout my years of ministry, standing in the shadows and offering prayers as I ascended the pulpit to preach the Word. Their presence has been a source of strength and encouragement, shaping my journey in profound ways. Among these unsung heroes of the faith are the church members who have gathered in my office to circle me in prayer before funerals, embodying the true spirit of community and support.

The individuals who have quietly prayed for me from the sidelines have played a significant role in sustaining me through the challenges and triumphs of ministry. Their unwavering faith and dedication have served as a constant reminder of the power of intercession and communal support within the body of believers. Whether it was a difficult sermon to deliver or a heartbreaking funeral to preside over, these precious souls have always been there, offering their prayers and presence without seeking recognition or praise.

The act of gathering around me in prayer before funerals has been a poignant display of the bond shared within the church community. As we joined hands and lifted our hearts in prayer, I could feel the strength and comfort of their support enveloping me, providing solace in moments of grief and loss. Their willingness to stand with me in those somber moments underscored the depth of their commitment to our shared faith and the importance of unity in times of sorrow.

In the tapestry of my ministry, these unsung heroes of the faith have woven threads of love, faith, and support that have enriched my journey beyond measure. Their prayers, their presence, and their unwavering commitment to standing with me in both joy and sorrow have been a constant source of inspiration and strength.

As I reflect on the impact they have had on my life and ministry, I am reminded of the profound truth that it is often those who work quietly behind the scenes that make the greatest difference. Every minister they've touched cherishes and celebrates these unsung heroes of the faith, whose contributions the world may overlook. God bless each of them in their faithfulness to His kingdom.

Scripture:

Philippians 1:3

"I thank my God upon every remembrance of you."

Devotional: "Those Who Serve"

Practicing gratitude is a powerful spiritual tool that improves our relationships and helps us live according to God's plan. Philippians 1:3 records Paul expressing heartfelt gratitude for his ministry's supporters. Let his words prompt us to appreciate the kindness, love, and support shown to us by others.

We've witnessed Jesus' compassion through the kindness of others. Their kindness and empathy highlight our unity in Christ. Expressing gratitude not only acknowledges others' contributions but also uplifts God, who uses them to bless us.

Let's nurture hearts brimming with thankfulness, expressing gratitude freely and happily. By doing this, we reinforce our loving bonds and mirror God's beautiful grace.

Prayer:

With grateful hearts, we thank You, Father, for the people in our lives. I appreciate their love, kindness, and support. Lord, shower them with Your blessings, peace, and presence. Help us to always see and value how You use others to bless us. May we honor them with our thanks and glorify You. In Jesus' name, Amen.

Reflective Questions:

1. Who are some people you are most thankful for in your life? How can you express your gratitude to them today?

2. How does showing gratitude to others deepen your relationship with God?

3. In what ways can you be a source of blessing and encouragement to others in your community?

38

THE INNOCENCE OF CHILDREN

Children's Innocence

Charles E. Cravey

A child's laughter, pure and bright,

Like sunbeams breaking through the night.

Their eyes aglow, a wondrous gaze,

A heart unspoiled by life's haze.

No burden bears their tender frame,

No greed, no pride, no worldly claim.

Their simple trust, their boundless love,

A gift bestowed from God above.

Oh, fleeting age of innocence sweet,

Where joy and truth and grace meet.

May we recall, may we relearn,

The childlike faith for which we yearn.

For in their steps, a glimpse divine,

God's kingdom shines through their design.

Their laughter calls, their spirits teach,

The depth of faith that we must reach.

There is a certain beauty about the innocence of children and their place in the church. Children bring a sense of purity and wonder to the church environment, reminding us of the simple faith and trust that we often lose as adults. Their presence can be a source of joy and inspiration, as they eagerly take part in church activities and rituals with enthusiasm.

Children also have a unique ability to ask questions and seek understanding, challenging us to deepen our own faith and knowledge. In a world that can sometimes feel jaded and cynical, the innocence of children in the church serves as a powerful reminder of the hope and light that faith can bring.

At our church, our pastor incorporates a Children's Moment in the Sunday service, where he invites the junior members of the congregation to take part. This special segment takes place at the altar and provides a platform for children to engage with the pastor and ask questions. It is heartwarming to see the innocence and curiosity of the children as they interact with our pastor.

The children's inquiries range from simple to spirited, with some posing challenging questions that spark thoughtful discussions. Our pastor handles these moments with grace and humor, often using what he calls "Kid Gloves" to address the children's inquiries with care and understanding.

The Children's Moment during our Sunday service is a cherished tradition that brings joy and laughter to our congregation. It is a beautiful reminder of the pure hearts and inquisitive minds of our junior members, and the pastor's gentle approach in responding to their questions with "Kid Gloves" exemplifies the love and respect we have for all members of our church community.

Scripture:

Matthew 19:14

"But Jesus said, Suffer little children, and forbid them not, to come unto me: for of such is the kingdom of heaven."

Devotional: Children are Precious

Children's innocence mirrors God's perfect purity and love. Matthew 19:14 highlights Jesus' emphasis on childlike faith, urging us to emulate children's humility, trust, and joy. Kids experience the world with awe and embrace life openly; traits that diminish with age and life's difficulties.

Children, in their faith, offer adults a model of complete trust in God, unconditional love, and daily joy in simple blessings. Their innocence highlights the need to safeguard and cultivate purity in their lives and our spiritual growth.

As we journey with Christ, let's cultivate childlike faith, for heaven welcomes the trusting and lighthearted.

Prayer:

Father, I thank you for our children and their innocent nature. Let their trust, joy, and humility be a lesson for us, and may we embody these virtues. Guide us to come to You with the innocent faith of a child, to love unconditionally, and to trust Your plan implicitly. Let us nurture our children's spirits and guide them towards Your truth. Amen.

Reflective Questions:

1. How does the innocence of children inspire your faith?

2. What steps can you take to nurture childlike qualities in your spiritual walk?

3. How can you protect and nurture the innocence of children in your life and community?

4. In what ways may you bless the children in your church?

39

A THIRST FOR RIGHTEOUSNESS

A Thirst for Righteousness

Charles E. Cravey

As deserts yearn for streams to flow,

My soul seeks what Your truths bestow.

A thirst for righteousness, so pure,

In You alone, I find the cure.

No worldly well can quench my need,

For living waters, Lord, I plead.

Each step, each prayer, a journey steep,

Your paths of truth, my soul, will keep.

Oh, hunger deep, no earthly fare,

Can satisfy the love You share.

In righteousness, my heart will grow.

Through grace, Your Spirit's touch will show.

So fill this cup, my Lord, my King,

With righteousness, let praises ring.

In seeking You, my thirst's released,

My soul finds rest, and my heart finds peace.

On my many trips along the Appalachian Trail, I have found myself and my scout team thirsty for the cool springs of water that gush out of the rocks. The crystal-clear water flowing from these natural springs has always been a source of refreshment and rejuvenation during our long hikes through the wilderness. To this day, I vividly remember the taste of that water being far superior to the tap water back home. Its purity and freshness are unmatched, making it a cherished memory of our adventures on the trail. The experience of drinking from these springs serves as a reminder of the beauty and abundance of nature that surrounds us.

In reflecting on our existence, it is crucial to acknowledge the innate human desire for righteousness. This fundamental aspect of our being serves as a reminder that there is a yearning within us for something greater than ourselves. It speaks to a deeper longing for moral integrity, justice, and fairness in our lives. This thirst for righteousness transcends individual desires and calls us to aspire towards a higher purpose, guiding our actions and decisions. Embracing this universal yearning can lead us towards personal growth, social harmony, and a more fulfilling existence. Let us recognize and nurture this thirst for righteousness within us as it propels us towards a life of purpose and meaning.

Scripture:

Matthew 5:6

Devotional: Thirst for Righteousness

To yearn for righteousness means desiring a life guided by God's principles of truth, justice, and love. In the Beatitudes, Matthew 5:6 promises satisfaction to those who yearn for righteousness.

This yearning surpasses a simple want. In a world filled with distractions and temptations, maintaining this hunger and thirst requires intentionality. This involves praying to God, studying the Bible, and trying to show God's love through our daily deeds.

Prioritizing righteousness brings a fulfillment from God that the world can't match. He sustains our spirits, fortifies our hearts, and bestows upon us a peace beyond comprehension. May our desire for Him and His righteousness never end, confident that He will meet our every need.

Prayer:

Lord, our hearts hunger, and our souls thirst for Your righteousness. Inspire us with Your Spirit, leading us toward truth and justice. Help us find You each day, treasure Your Word, and live in a way that shows Your grace. May our desire for You intensify daily, bringing us joy and purpose in Your presence. In Jesus' name, Amen.

Reflective Questions:

1. What does it mean to you to hunger and thirst after righteousness?

2. How can you nurture your spiritual hunger and stay focused on God's will?

3. In what ways can pursuing righteousness bring peace and joy to your life?

40

My Faith Looks Up to Thee

My Faith Looks Up

Charles E. Cravey

My faith looks up beyond the skies,

To where eternal blessings lie.

A beacon bright. Your light does shine,

O Lord, my Savior, guide divine.

Through trials deep and valleys low,

Your grace sustains, Your mercies flow.

Though storms may rage, my heart will rest.

In You, my refuge, I am blessed.

No fear can shake, no doubt consumes,

Your steadfast love dispels the gloom.

My faith endures, my eyes will see,

The hope fulfilled; my soul set free.

So let me walk my hand in Thine,

Through every path, Your will aligns.

My faith looks up, secure and true.

O Lord, I place my trust in You.

The worst rainstorm I've ever endured was in a small cabin in the North Carolina mountains with my wife, Renee. Torrential rain, the heaviest I'd ever seen, flooded the area outside our cabin and sent rushing water cascading down all night. The thunder roared louder than ever before as mountains surrounded us. The lightning seemed to pierce through the house and into our hearts as we huddled upstairs in the loft bed, said a prayer, and eventually drifted off to sleep. What a night we will not soon forget!

We've all endured the storms of life, haven't we? Some have been mild, but many have been hard. The resilience we have in times like these tests our spirit and causes us to lean on the Almighty for comfort. Luckily, Renee and I had each other, knowing that God had us.

The following morning, Renee and I awoke to a scene of devastation outside. The storm uprooted trees and strewn them across the landscape, leaving power lines dangerously on the ground and leaving us without electricity. Fallen debris completely blocked the road we had traveled to reach our destination, preventing our departure until emergency crews cleared it later that day. Eager to escape the chaos and destruction, Renee and I wasted no time in getting out of that place as soon as it was safe to do so.

I'm sure you have witnessed such storms in your life, whether they were weather-related or spiritual. How we manage getting through the storms depends solely on our faith in God. Trust him. He will see you through.

Scripture:

Hebrews 12:2

"Looking unto Jesus the author and finisher of our faith; who for the joy that was set before him endured the cross, despising the shame, and is set down at the right hand of the throne of God."

Devotional: "My Faith Looks Up to Thee"

"My Faith Looks Up to Thee" powerfully expresses trust and hope. Faith doesn't prevent life's storms; it grounds us in the One who stills them. Hebrews 12:2 encourages us to focus on Jesus, the founder and perfecter of our faith.

Faith is a journey of reliance, where we transcend our limitations and submit to God's plan. When we look up and trust completely, we feel God's strength, peace, and guidance.

Let's cling to our faith; may it always strengthen and support us through every challenge. Looking to Him in faith reminds us of His enduring, unfailing love and promises.

Prayer:

O Lord, in You, our faith finds its source of hope and strength. Help us trust You completely, to rely on Your strength, and to walk confidently, secure in Your presence. May our faith, grounded in Your Word and love, become unwavering and genuine. Lead us every step, keeping our focus on You. Amen.

Reflective Questions:

1. What does it mean for your faith to "look up" to Jesus in times of difficulty?

2. How can you grow in your trust and dependence on God daily?

3. In what ways does fixing your eyes on Jesus bring peace and strength to your life?

4. What are some notable storms you have been through in your personal life?

41

THE DARK NIGHT OF THE SOUL

"The Dark Night of the Soul"

Charles E. Cravey

Amid the hush of the olive grove,

The Savior knelt, His love to prove.

A night of anguish, tears that fell,

The weight of sin is a heavy spell.

His trembling voice rose to the skies.

Through solemn plea and mournful cries.

"Let this cup pass," His heart implored.

Yet still He bowed, the cross adored.

In shadows deep, the tempter's gaze,

A battle fought in mercy's haze.

Sweat like blood adorned His brow.

The hour was near, redemption's vow.

Forsaken path, yet love's embrace,

He bore our burden in that space.

Through agony, His light did shine.

Eternal grace, a gift divine.

The darkened hour, the silent plea,

Revealed the depths of love's decree.

O night of sorrow, hope concealed,

Through sacrifice, salvation was sealed.

I've often wondered about the pain and agony of Jesus as he knelt in the darkness of Gethsemane that night of his arrest. As he grappled with the knowledge of the suffering and sacrifice awaiting him, the weight of what was to come must have felt unbearable. The silence of the garden would have been deafening, broken only by his anguished prayers to the Father. The mental and emotional turmoil he experienced in that moment is beyond comprehension, as he faced the ultimate test of his faith and purpose. Reflecting on this profound moment in Jesus' life reminds us of the depth of his love and the extent of his sacrifice for all of humanity.

Life is a journey filled with various challenges and obstacles that can lead us to face our "dark nights of the soul." Profound grief, intense pain, and overwhelming emotions often characterize these moments. A myriad of experiences can trigger them, such as losing a loved one, facing serious surgery, or the unimaginable tragedy of losing a child. The list of potential triggers for these dark nights is long and varied, highlighting the unpredictability and complexity of life's trials. Despite the deep suffering that accompanies these dark nights, they also offer opportunities for growth, resilience, and transformation. It is in these moments of darkness that we are called to confront our deepest fears, face our vulnerabilities, and emerge stronger and more compassionate individuals.

Scripture:

Matthew 26:38-39

"Then saith he unto them, My soul is exceeding sorrowful, even unto death: tarry ye here, and watch with me. And he went a little farther, and fell on his face, and prayed, saying, O my Father, if it be possible, let this cup pass from me: nevertheless not as I will, but as thou wilt."

Devotional: "The Dark Night of the Soul"

The Garden of Gethsemane marks one of the most poignant moments in Jesus' earthly journey, often referred to as His "dark night of the soul." Here, He bore the weight of humanity's sin and faced the anguish of separation from the Father. It was a night of surrender, where divine love triumphed over fear and sorrow. In life's darkest moments, we too grapple with pain, uncertainty, and the call to surrender. Jesus' prayer, "Not my will, but Thine," invites us to trust God's plan, even when the path seems unbearable. His willingness to face the cross out of love for humanity assures us we are never alone, even in our deepest struggles.

The Garden teaches us the power of prayer, the comfort of surrender, and the hope that light follows even the darkest night. As we walk through our own seasons of Gethsemane, may we remember Jesus walking with us, offering strength and peace. In times of trial and tribulation, the story of Jesus in the Garden of Gethsemane serves as a powerful reminder of the importance of faith, surrender, and perseverance. Just as Jesus trusted in God's plan despite the immense challenges before Him, we, too, can draw strength from His example and find solace knowing that we are never alone in our struggles. Let us take comfort in the lessons of Gethsemane and embrace the transformative power of surrendering our will to God's, knowing that His love and grace will guide us through even the darkest of nights.

Prayer:

Father, when sorrow and fear grip us, remind us of Your constant love. Guide us to have faith in Your plan, despite not comprehending it fully. Help us learn to surrender as Jesus did in the Garden, saying, "Not my will, but Yours." Give us strength during our challenges and provide us with the unique peace that only comes from You. We thank You for Jesus' ultimate sacrifice; He endured the darkest night to bring us into Your glorious light.

In Jesus' name, we pray, Amen.

Reflective Questions:

1. What does surrendering your will to God look like in your own life?

2. How can Jesus' prayer in Gethsemane inspire you during times of trial?

3. In what ways do you find comfort knowing that Jesus fully understands human suffering?

4. How can prayer help you navigate your "dark night of the soul"?

42

THE GREATEST GIFT

"The Greatest Gift"

Charles E. Cravey

Upon the earth, a humble birth,

A King descended, clothed in mirth.

Through the manger's straw and night's embrace,

He came to save the human race.

Not wrapped in silk, nor crowned with gold,

But love more vast than hearts can hold.

The gift of grace, unearned, divine,

Eternal life through love's design.

For God so loved, the Scriptures sing,

He gave His Son, our risen King.

No greater gift could heaven bestow,

Than Christ, who conquered death's cruel woe.

The perfect Lamb, our sin He bore,

His sacrifice is an open door.

O precious gift, beyond all measure,

God's boundless love, our lasting treasure.

The greatest gift bestowed upon humanity was the precious Christ child, given to Mary and Joseph as a symbol of hope and salvation. This miraculous event marked the beginning of a new chapter in history, offering the promise of redemption and eternal grace to all who believe. The birth of Jesus Christ not only brought joy to his earthly parents but also to the world, serving as a beacon of light in times of darkness.

As we reflect on this divine gift, let us remember God's boundless love and mercy, shown to us through his son's birth. The birth of Jesus Christ is a profound moment in human history that continues to inspire faith and hope across generations. This miraculous event, celebrated by billions around the world, symbolizes the ultimate act of love and grace from a benevolent God.

The story of Jesus' birth in Bethlehem, as told in the Gospels of Matthew and Luke, highlights the humble circumstances of the Son of God. Born in a manger, surrounded by animals, and visited by shepherds and wise men, Jesus entered the world as a vulnerable infant, yet destined for greatness. The significance of Christ's birth lies in its message of redemption and salvation for all humanity. Through his teachings and ultimate sacrifice, Jesus offered a path to eternal life and forgiveness of sins, embodying God's unconditional love for humanity.

As we commemorate the birth of Jesus Christ each year, let's recall this divine gift's profound impact on our lives. May we embrace the message of hope, love, and salvation that Christ brings and strive to live according to his teachings of compassion, forgiveness, and faith. The miracle of Christ's birth is a timeless reminder of God's boundless love and mercy towards his creation.

Scripture:

John 3:16

"For God so loved the world, that he gave his only begotten Son, that whosoever believeth in him should not perish, but have everlasting life."

Devotional: "The Greatest Gift"

John 3:16 perfectly summarizes God's immeasurable love: "For God so loved the world that he gave his only begotten Son." Jesus Christ's sacrifice atones for our sins and promises everlasting life.

This gift isn't materially extravagant; its richness lies in humility, grace, and unconditional love. Jesus' earthly mission was to offer salvation, a free gift to all believers. Let's contemplate God's immeasurable love, remembering the sacrifice and His profound compassion for us.

Nothing limits this amazing gift to a specific time of year. God's gift of Christ to the world made redemption, hope, and everlasting peace possible. Let's cherish, share, and gratefully live each day with this precious gift.

Prayer:

Heavenly Father, we give thanks for Your unparalleled gift—Jesus Christ, Your Son. Through Him, You showed the depth of Your love, and He gave us salvation. Let's always appreciate this gift and live each day with thankfulness and obedience. Guide us to spread Your love and live according to Your eternal truth.

In Jesus' name, Amen.

Reflective Questions:

1. How does understanding God's love through Jesus change your perspective on life?

2. What are ways you can share "the greatest gift" with others?

3. How does recognizing the value of this gift influence your daily walk with Christ?

4. How can gratitude for Jesus' sacrifice transform your attitude in challenging times?

43

SACRED STILLNESS

Sacred Stillness

Charles E. Cravey

In the muted dawn, where shadows play,

A glimmer of hope ignites the day.

Through trials and tears, faith takes flight,

Guided gently by love's soft light.

The storms may rage, the winds may roar,

But within the heart lies something more.

A seed of grace, a whisper divine,

That blossoms when the soul aligns.

Each step we take, though paths unclear,

Is etched with purpose, free from fear.

The journey twists, the valleys deep,

Yet mercy's promise wakes from sleep.

So, rise anew, O weary soul,

For boundless peace shall make you whole.

In sacred stillness, truth is found,

And heaven's grace shall then abound.

I find immense value in the tranquility of my daily routine. The peaceful environment around me acts as a catalyst for my creativity and introspection. Amidst the hustle and bustle that engulfs so many individuals, I take refuge in my serene writing space. Here, I can focus without distractions, allowing my thoughts to flow freely and my ideas to take shape. Though occasionally interrupted by the ringing of the phone, these moments of quiet reflection are essential for my inspiration and insight.

In the serene embrace of a quiet space, my mind becomes a canvas for a flood of thoughts and ideas waiting to be expressed. With a sense of divine guidance, I swiftly jot down my articles and devotionals, capturing the essence of inspiration before it slips away. In this precious moment, time is of the essence, leaving little room for distractions or frivolities except for the simple joy of walking my beloved Boykin Spaniel.

Comfortably, I interpret the world from my perspective. I hope others can also have this quiet time and use it wisely. Schedule some personal time each day for prayer and reflection. You will eventually understand how valuable these moments are.

Scripture:

Isaiah 40:31

"But those who hope in the Lord will renew their strength. They will soar on wings like eagles; they will run and not grow weary, they will walk and not be faint."

Devotional: "Renewal and Hope"

Life is an ongoing series of transformations—a blend of triumphs and setbacks, serenity and chaos. In this cycle of change, renewal is a blessing from God, inherent in our lives. No matter how dark the night, dawn will always come, reminding us of this.

We encounter renewal in numerous ways. Other times, it's a slow, unfolding process, much like a flower blooming. Imagine a caterpillar, encased in a cocoon, abandoned by the world. Miraculously, it becomes a butterfly, symbolizing transformation and hope through an unseen process. Similarly, God's work in our lives might be invisible, yet equally magnificent.

The Bible instructs us to trust God's timing. We might feel tired and unsure if we're strong enough to overcome this. However, Isaiah 40:31 gives us this comfort: "Those who wait for the Lord will regain their power." They will soar on wings like eagles; they will run and not grow weary, they will walk and not be faint." This verse is a promise that renewal is not just a possibility—it's inevitable when we lean into God's grace.

Prayer and reflection renew our souls in their sacred stillness. Silence is not a void. When we listen, we discover peace that surpasses understanding. We are always in God's hands, regardless of what challenges we face.

Renewal serves as a call to action. God's renewal empowers us to renew others. How do you give hope to a hopeless person? In what ways can you show God's mercy and grace in your daily life? Spreading the message of renewal improves your life and the lives of those near you.

Today, accept renewal as both a gift and a duty. Trust in God's guidance as you move forward in faith. Even if you don't see the complete picture, trust in His plan's beauty. Let boundless love renew your soul and fill your heart with hope.

Prayer:

Heavenly Father, I thank you for your constant love and faithfulness. When life weighs me down, remind me You are my strength and refuge. Revive my spirit and allow Your guidance to fill my heart. Help me find peace in quiet moments and have faith in Your design, even when my future's unclear. May my actions inspire hope in those around me, reflecting your light. Amen.

Reflective Questions:

1. When was the last time you felt renewed spiritually, emotionally, or physically?

2. How can you cultivate moments of stillness in your daily routine to better connect with God?

3. Are there areas in your life where you need to trust in God's timing?

4. How can you share the message of renewal and hope with others around you?

44

FAITH THROUGH TRIALS

Faith Through Trials

Charles E. Cravey

When shadows fall and pathways veer,

And doubt brings whispers we long to clear,

A steadfast anchor holds us tight.

Guided by love through the darkest night.

The trials we face, though fierce they seem,

Are but threads in God's eternal scheme.

Through fire, our spirits are refined,

A treasure of faith eternally aligned.

Though storms may lash, our souls still stand,

Upheld by grace, by His mighty hand.

For every tear, a seed shall grow,

A harvest of joy the world will know.

So, fear not the valleys, deep and wide,

For God is with us, our faithful guide.

In trials, His strength becomes our song.

Our faith is enduring, unwavering, and strong.

Mabel adored her life and her family, which were growing. She joyfully cared for her two children, the second of whom had recently arrived. Unexpectedly, news arrived one morning that shattered her world; her husband's company downsized, resulting in his unemployment.

Initially, panic overcame Mabel. Facing mounting bills and the need to provide for my family, the future seemed bleak and daunting. A sense of dread filled her as she questioned their survival. Mabel's vulnerability brought back her grandmother's words: "Faith doesn't mean there won't be storms.

Rather than succumbing to despair, Mabel sought solace in prayer. Every morning, she'd wake before her family, pray at her bedside, and confide in God. Matthew 6:26, "Look at the birds of the air," brought her solace. "Aren't you far more valuable than them?"

To overcome their challenges, Mabel and her husband started taking small, consistent steps. With a revised budget, church community support, and unwavering faith, they persevered. An inexplicable peace settled over Mabel, even amidst bleak prospects. She knew God was in their midst, no matter what happened.

Mabel's husband finally landed a new job after months of trying. The position was anything but ordinary. Looking back, Mabel realized that the trial she feared had strengthened her faith and brought her closer to God. It showed how faith in Him can change inconvenient situations into chances to grow.

Scripture:

James 1:2-4

"Consider it pure joy, my brothers and sisters, whenever you face trials of many kinds, because you know that the testing of your faith produces perseverance. Let perseverance finish its work so that you may be mature and complete, not lacking anything."

Devotional: Faith Through Trials

Trials make faith most clear. Just as a potter carefully shapes clay, God uses challenges to mold us into resilient and purposeful individuals. Trials don't mean God has abandoned you.

Consider how gold is refined. Intense heat refines the ore, removing impurities to reveal its true brilliance. Hardship tests and strengthens our faith in the same manner. God uses our pain to create beauty. Every challenge is an opportunity to trust in His power and let go of our anxieties.

James 1:2-4 urges us to greet trials with joy, for they build perseverance. Though it may seem illogical during this turmoil, have faith that God's vision encompasses the greater context. Obstacles and detours are part of God's plan to prepare you for future blessings.

Walking through trials with faith reveals God's boundless love and provision. Unlike a distant observer, he's always there to help when things get tough. Cling to His promises; may your heart overflow with a peace beyond all comprehension.

Prayer:

Gracious Father, during my trials, I seek Your guidance. Bolster my belief and reaffirm that You are my haven and stronghold. When burdens become overwhelming, help me find solace in Your steadfast love. Mold me through my struggles so that I may radiate Your glory. Help me view every challenge as a chance to draw nearer to You and to have faith in Your flawless plan. Thanks for always being there for me during tough times. Amen.

Reflective Questions:

1. What challenges in your life have strengthened your faith over time?

2. How do you typically respond to trials? Is there a way to shift your perspective toward seeing them as opportunities for growth?

3. Are there specific scriptures or stories that have brought you comfort during challenging times?

4. How can you support someone else who is facing a trial of their own?

45

A HEART OF GRATITUDE

Gratitude

Charles E. Cravey

In the morning's light, soft and true,

Gratitude whispers, calling you.

For blessings seen, for gifts concealed,

A thankful heart is fully healed.

The song of the birds, the rustling trees,

The quiet strength in every breeze,

Each moment shouts of grace divine,

A sacred echo, a holy sign.

Gratitude blooms like a flower in spring,

A melody only the humble can sing.

Through trials and triumphs, it takes its stand,

A gift held gently in God's own hand.

So, pause and breathe, and look around,

For countless treasures still abound.

With grateful hearts, we'll rise and see,

The beauty of eternity.

"We need an attitude of gratitude." In our fast-paced and often chaotic world, it is easy to get caught up in negativity and stress. However, by cultivating a mindset of gratitude, we can shift our focus towards the positive aspects of our lives. Practicing gratitude involves acknowledging and appreciating the blessings, big or small, that we encounter each day. It can improve our mental and emotional well-being, enhance our relationships, and even boost our overall happiness. So, let us strive to embrace an attitude of gratitude in all aspects of our lives.

Scripture:

I Thessalonians 5:18

"Give thanks in all circumstances; for this is God's will for you in Christ Jesus."

Devotional: Gratitude

Gratitude is deeper than a temporary emotion. In a culture that often focuses on what we lack, choosing gratitude allows us to focus on the countless blessings we already possess.

Gratitude alters our hearts. This changes our viewpoint from a lack of resources to an abundance of them and from worry to confidence. In 1 Thessalonians 5:18, Paul instructs us to give thanks always during both good and bad times. Feeling thankful during difficult times isn't ignoring problems; it's trusting God's plan, even if we can't see it.

Being thankful also puts us in harmony with God's plan. Acknowledging God's sovereignty over our lives comes from thanking Him for both big and small blessings. Gratitude cultivates humility, joy, and contentment, preparing us to be vessels of God's work.

Pause and reflect for a moment today. What recent blessings have you received from God? Maybe you've missed some blessings; which ones? Cultivating gratitude reveals profound gifts in simple moments like sunlight and smiles, reminding you of His love.

Prayer:

God, I thank You for Your countless blessings in my life. Help me cultivate gratitude, even when things get tough. Help me appreciate the beauty of Your creation and Your daily kindness. Guide me to trust Your plans and be thankful for Your direction, even when I cannot see the path ahead. May my thankfulness spread to others, mirroring Your kindness and affection. Amen.

Reflective Questions:

1. What are three things you're grateful for today?

2. How can practicing gratitude change your outlook on challenges you're facing?

3. Do you regularly thank God for the small blessings in life, as well as the big ones?

46

GRACE

Unbounded Grace

Charles E. Cravey

Unmerited, boundless, a gift so pure,

Grace flows freely, steadfast, and sure.

Not earned by works, nor bought by gold,

A love eternal, unbroken, bold.

It finds the sinner, the lost, the weak,

Lifting the weary, giving voice to the meek.

Through trials faced and paths unclear,

Grace whispers softly, "I'm always here."

When guilt's shadow looms, heavy and wide,

Grace steps in to turn the tide.

A bridge to hope, a balm for pain,

Through grace, we're born anew again.

So, rest in grace; let your heart release.

Its boundless mercy brings perfect peace.

A gift divine, no strings, no cost,

Redeeming love for the broken and lost.

People frequently characterize grace as unearned and freely given. This concept surpasses human comprehension; it embodies selfless kindness, forgiveness, and love. Grace is a freely given gift, unconditional and without requirements. In times of need, it offers comfort, strength, and hope. Finding grace brings peace and acceptance, assuring one of unconditional love and value. Grace embodies the inherent goodness and generosity of the world, illuminating even the darkest times.

Kindness, forgiveness, love, and compassion are just some examples of grace found throughout life. You can find it in small everyday gestures like a stranger's smile or a friend's helping hand. Nature, with its beautiful sunrises and tranquil forests, also embodies grace. Grace, in its essence, embodies humanity's finest qualities, shining brightly wherever goodness and positivity exist.

Scripture:

Romans 5:8

"But God demonstrates His own love for us in this: While we were still sinners, Christ died for us."

Devotional: Grace: The Heartbeat of the Gospel

Grace is the core of the gospel—a free, undeserved, and unparalleled gift. God's immeasurable love extends to us, especially during our struggles, empowering us to achieve things beyond our individual capabilities. Grace doesn't expect perfection from us.

Romans 5:8 highlights grace's beauty: Christ's death wasn't deserved, but an act of boundless love. This is grace at its most pure: sacrificial, abundant, and steadfast. This bridge connects our humanity to God's divinity.

Grace offers freedom, too. It breaks the chains of guilt and shame, replacing them with forgiveness and renewal. God's love always surrounds us, no matter how lost we may feel.

Reflecting on grace's role in your life, ask yourself: How often do you accept it completely? Are you equally forgiving towards others? Grace is more than just something to accept. In living a life marked by grace, we reflect the very heart of God.

Prayer:

Gracious Father, thank you for your loving grace—a profound love encompassing my imperfections, raising me to new heights. Guide me to accept this gift completely, allowing it to change my heart and direct my path. Help me show grace to others, mirroring Your compassion and mercy in everything I do. Grant me the freedom and joy Your grace offers, always mindful of Christ's sacrifice. So be it.

Reflective Questions:

1. When have you experienced God's grace when you least expected

it?

2. Are there areas in your life where guilt or shame prevents you from fully receiving God's grace?

3. How can you show grace to someone who needs it today?

4. What does living a life marked by grace mean to you personally?

PRAYING FOR MY PASTOR

My Shepherd Leads

Charles E. Cravey

A shepherd walks with steadfast care,

Through trials and burdens, unaware.

Their hands extend, their hearts embrace,

A vessel of love, a source of grace.

Yet even the strong can tire and weep,

For the path is long, the valleys deep.

A pastor's journey, though guided by light,

Needs prayers to strengthen them through the fight.

So, lift them high, in prayer and deed,

Ask God to meet their every need.

For as they serve, so must we,

To stand beside them faithfully.

As I reflect on my fifty-year tenure as a pastor, I am overwhelmed by the countless prayers people offered on my behalf. Throughout the highs and lows of my ministry, the support and intercession of others have been a source of strength and encouragement. These prayers have carried me through challenging times, sustained me in moments of doubt, and lifted me up in times of celebration. I am deeply grateful for the individuals and communities who have faithfully prayed for me over the years, and I am humbled by the power of collective prayer in sustaining my journey as a pastor.

Today, my wife and I pray daily for our two ministers, asking God to guide them righteously. We hold them dear and pray God grants them vision and strength to fulfill His will in our church and community. Start a prayer ministry for your pastor today; it's a great idea.

Scripture:

1 Timothy 5:17

"The elders who direct the affairs of the church well are worthy of double honor, especially those whose work is preaching and teaching."

Devotional: "For Those Who Serve"

Pastors, as shepherds of God's flock, should lead with wisdom, compassion, and strength. However, their role presents some challenges. A human being, burdened by the responsibility of guiding others, hides beneath the sermons, prayers, and tireless service. Despite offering support, they require encouragement, rest, and spiritual renewal as well.

1 Timothy 5:17 highlights the honor and respect due to pastors. Prayer is one of the most effective ways we can help them. Supporting your pastor through prayer isn't merely an act of goodwill; it's a collaborative effort in ministry. This harmonizes your heart with God's plan and fortifies the connection between shepherd and flock.

Ask for wisdom, safety, and peace for them and their families. Seek strength in times of uncertainty and perseverance during difficult periods. Prayer is good, but show your thankfulness through words and actions, too. Show appreciation for their hard work and sacrifices.

Your prayers are a source of strength for your pastor, supporting their ministry and strengthening their faith. Let's stand together as a church family, united in faith and supporting our leaders with love.

Prayer:

We thank God for our pastor's faithful guidance and service to our church. I'm lifting them up to You today, seeking Your protection, strength, and wisdom. Revive their spirits, bringing them joy and peace as they follow Your purpose. Protect their hearts from discouragement and build a supportive community around them. Pray continually for them, and help me show my gratitude for their service. Shower their ministry and family with Your blessings and let them experience the immensity of Your love. Amen.

Reflective Questions:

1. How often do you pray for your pastor and their family?

2. In what ways can you offer encouragement to your pastor beyond prayer?

3. Are there challenges your pastor might face that you can support through service or kindness?

4. How can you lead by example in fostering a culture of prayer for church leaders?

48

NEW YEAR'S

A NEW YEAR

Charles E. Cravey

The clock strikes twelve, a chapter closed.

A year gone by, its tale composed.

Through joys and trials, we stand anew,

With hearts refreshed and skies in view.

The dawn unfolds, a gift unknown.

A path to walk where seeds are sown.

God's hand shall guide, His grace shall steer,

With steadfast love through the coming year.

So lift your gaze, let go of fear,

Embrace the moments of this year.

For every step is marked with care,

In His promise, we're forever there.

We stand on the threshold of a brand-new year, filled with endless possibilities and opportunities. We haven't written its script yet, but you can shape it with your actions and choices. What will you make of it? Would you like to seize the moment and do something truly inspiring, or will you let the days slip by in trivial living? Each new day of this year presents an open book for you to write, with blank pages waiting to be filled with your dreams, goals, and achievements. Embrace the unknown, embrace the challenges, and embrace the potential that lies within you to make this year your best one yet. God bless you on your journey.

Scripture:

Isaiah 43:18-19

"Forget the former things; do not dwell on the past. See, I am doing a new thing! Now it springs up; do you not perceive it? I am making a way in the wilderness and streams in the wasteland."

Devotional: NEW YEAR'S

The New Year's arrival signifies God's promise of renewal and transformation. Isaiah 43:18–19 beautifully depicts God's invitation to leave the past behind and embrace His current work in our lives. The new year is a blank canvas, full of potential, created by God.

Our past mistakes and regrets do not limit God. He persistently works, creating solutions where there appear to be none—providing resources in our barren areas. This New Year, refocus your heart and trust in God's perfect plan. As you set intentions, trust in His guidance and love, knowing God divinely directs each step.

In the coming year, resolve to spend time with Him each day. Seek His presence in moments of quiet reflection, and let His Word be a lamp to your feet and a light to your path. Whether the year brings joy, trials, or unexpected surprises, trust that God is with you every step of the way.

Prayer:

Father in Heaven, we give thanks for this New Year, a season for reflection, renewal, and faith in Your word. Guide me to release past hurts and move forward with trust. Show me the path and the plans You have for my future. Guide my decisions to honor You and fill my heart with joy and hope as I follow Your path. May this year show Your unwavering faithfulness and grace. Amen.

Reflective Questions:

1. What are three blessings from the past year that you are most thankful for?

2. Are there areas in your life where you need to trust God's plan more deeply in the coming year?

3. What spiritual practices or commitments can you make this year to grow closer to God?

4. How can you bring His light into your community as you start the new year?

49

EASTER

---◆❖◆---

Christ Has Opened Heaven's Door

Charles E. Cravey

The stone was rolled; the tomb laid bare.

A breath of life, triumph declared.

From death to hope, the Savior rose,

The gift of grace, His love, bestows.

The cross once bore the weight of pain,

Yet through it shines eternal gain.

For every tear, for every sin,

His blood redeemed, new life begins.

Rejoice, O hearts, let voices soar,

For Christ has opened heaven's door.

A risen King, our faith restored,

Forevermore, He is adored.

Easter must be my favorite time of the year. Spring has sprung in all its grandeur and beauty. My yard is a plethora of colors as new buds and blooms pop everywhere! Bluebirds are finding their new nesting places in my bluebird boxes, and life is good. As the season transitions from the cold grasp of winter to the warm embrace of spring, nature comes alive in a symphony of colors and sounds. The vibrant hues of tulips, daffodils, and hyacinths paint a picture of renewal and hope. The sweet fragrance of blossoms fills the air, a gentle reminder of the beauty that surrounds us.

Amidst this colorful tapestry, bluebirds flit about, their cheerful songs echoing through the garden. I watch with delight as they build their nests in the bluebird boxes I carefully placed around the yard. It warms my heart to see new life taking root in my little corner of the world.

As Easter approaches, I am filled with a sense of gratitude for the beauty that surrounds me. It is a time of reflection and renewal, a time to appreciate the wonders of nature and the simple joys of life. In this season of rebirth, I am reminded of the importance of embracing the beauty that is all around us, and I am grateful for the opportunity to witness it firsthand in my backyard. To God be the glory!

Scripture:

Matthew 28:6

"He is not here; he has risen, just as he said. Come and see the place where he lay."

Devotional: Victory Over Death

Easter gloriously celebrates Christ's triumph over death. God fulfills his promise. Representing resurrection, redemption, hope, and new beginnings, the empty tomb holds significance for believers.

In the angel's announcement in Matthew 28:6, it stated, "He is not here." Easter reminds us that no matter how heavy our burdens or how dark our seasons, there is always hope in Christ. His rising from the dead shows God's limitless love and ability to conquer death.

Easter also compels us to live by this truth. How should we understand what "resurrection people" signify? This involves accepting Christ's forgiveness, confidently living your faith, and spreading the gospel. Like the women at the tomb, we're to spread the news of His love and grace.

May the Easter joy fill your heart. Celebrate the Savior's victory over death, granting us eternal life. Live each day celebrating the risen King's victory and promise.

Prayer:

Risen Lord, we thank You for Your sacrifice and the victory of Your resurrection. May Easter's hope and joy fill my heart, guiding me to live as a testament to Your love. Help me accept Your forgiveness and live freely through Your grace. Let my life shine with Your light, glorifying Your name and inspiring hope in others. Amen.

Reflective Questions:

1. How does the resurrection of Christ impact your faith and daily life?

2. Are there areas in your life where you need to embrace the promise

of new beginnings?

3. How can you share the message of Easter with someone who needs hope?

4. What are practical ways to live as a reflection of resurrection joy and grace?

———⬥✦⬥———

50

INDEPENDENCE DAY

Liberty's Call

Charles E. Cravey

A nation born from courage and fire,

Dreams of freedom, hearts aspire.

Through trials faced, a bond was made,

In unity strong, foundations laid.

The stars and stripes, a banner of grace,

A symbol of hope in every place.

For liberty's call, both loud and clear,

Is cherished by those who hold it dear.

O grateful hearts lift prayers high,

For the gift of freedom under God's sky.

May we walk in truth, with justice strong,

Together as one, where all belong.

Independence Day is a significant celebration in America, observed on the 4th of July every year. This holiday commemorates the Declaration of Independence in 1776, when the United States officially became an independent nation. People mark the day with various festivities, including parades, fireworks displays, barbecues, picnics, and concerts. It is a time for Americans to come together, show their patriotism, and honor the history and values of their country. Many cities and towns across the nation hold their own unique events to celebrate Independence Day, making it one of the most cherished holidays in America.

Scripture:

II Corinthians 3:17

"Now the Lord is the Spirit, and where the Spirit of the Lord is, there is freedom."

Devotional: Unity and Freedom

Independence Day is about more than just fireworks and celebrations; it's a time to reflect on our freedoms and the sacrifices that secured them. Our national identity is built on the sacrifices of those who fought for liberty and justice; however, only God can grant true freedom.

2 Corinthians 3:17 teaches us that the Spirit gifts us freedom. This freedom isn't just about happiness and belief; it's the liberation found in Christ, who shatters the bonds of sin and gives new life. While celebrating our nation's blessings, let's remember the true freedom found in His truth.

Unity also underpins independence. National strength arises from unity, shared purpose, and mutual love among its citizens. Similarly, as Christians, our calling is to live in unity, mutually supporting each other, and striving for the common good.

This Independence Day, express gratitude to God for your freedoms. Ask for guidance, unity, and justice for your nation's leaders and people. Remember, as citizens of this nation and God's kingdom, we are to protect His truth and love.

Prayer:

Lord, I thank You for the freedom I enjoy as a citizen and as Your child. This Independence Day, I pray for my country. May its leaders be wise, its people united, and may we all live justly and compassionately. Guide me to shine Your truth and love within my community. Let us value the liberties granted to us and use them to glorify You. Amen.

Reflective Questions:

1. How can you use the freedoms you enjoy reflecting God's love to others?

2. In what ways can you pray for and support unity within your community or nation?

3. What does spiritual freedom in Christ mean to you personally?

4. How can you honor the sacrifices of those who fought for freedom while living out your faith?

51

THANKSGIVING

Thankful Hearts

Charles E. Cravey

Golden fields, the harvest bright,

A table set in autumn's light.

Hands clasped in prayer, hearts full of grace,

For blessings poured in this sacred space.

Through trials faced, and storms endured,

God's love prevails, steadfast, assured.

With gratitude deep, we lift our voice,

In His provision, we rejoice.

O thankful hearts, embrace the day,

Let gratitude guide our words and ways.

For every gift, for mercy shown,

We praise the Lord, our cornerstone.

Thanksgiving is a special time of the year when we come together to give thanks to God, our Father, who lovingly provides for all our needs. It is a time to reflect on the blessings and abundance in our lives and to express gratitude for all that we have. Thanksgiving is a time of celebration, family gatherings, and sharing meals with loved ones. It is a time to count our blessings and to remember the importance of gratitude in our lives. This Thanksgiving, as we gather around the table, let's express gratitude for everything we have received and show appreciation for our many blessings.

Scripture:

Psalm 107:1

"Give thanks to the Lord, for He is good; His love endures forever."

Devotional: "Thanksgiving"

During Thanksgiving, we should pause and reflect on God's many blessings. It's not just a holiday; it's a chance to grow a grateful heart that lasts. Psalm 107:1 shows us God's goodness and unfailing love, providing for us throughout the year.

Being thankful changes how we see things. We can better see God's hand in life's difficulties because of it. Expressing gratitude for our blessings is easy, but we must also be thankful during struggles, trusting God's plan, even when it's unclear.

Thanksgiving is also an opportunity to appreciate our community's blessings. The gathering of loved ones around the table emphasizes fellowship. Sharing a meal reflects God's generosity in inviting us to His table and nourishing our souls.

During your Thanksgiving celebration, remember to acknowledge all that you're thankful for, regardless of size. Let the practice of gratitude enrich each day, changing your heart and relationships. God's unfailing love lasts eternally, regardless.

Prayer:

Thank you, gracious Father, for your unending love and many blessings. This Thanksgiving, I express my heartfelt gratitude to you. Guide me to find Your goodness in every moment and trust You during every trial. We ask for Your blessing on this time spent with family and friends; may Your presence fill our gathering. Help me live each day with the thankful spirit of Thanksgiving, showing Your grace and love to others. Amen.

Reflective Questions:

1. What are three specific blessings you're thankful for this year?

2. How can gratitude transform the way you view challenges in your life?

3. In what ways can you share God's blessings with someone in need during Thanksgiving?

4. How can you practice daily gratitude beyond this holiday?

52

CHRISTMAS

What Christmas Means

Charles E. Cravey

In Bethlehem's quiet, beneath the star's light,

A Savior was born on a holy night.

The angels rejoiced, their voices raised,

Glory to God, forever praised.

In a manger low, the King did lie,

Bringing hope to earth from heaven's sky.

The gift of love, so freely given,

A bridge of grace 'tween earth and heaven.

O hearts, behold this wondrous scene,

The miracle of what Christmas means.

Through Christ, the light of the world has come,

Emmanuel, God's only Son.

In a world of turmoil and strife, where uncertainty and unrest are the norm, a Savior enters our existence and calms the storm. Christmas, the grandest of all celebrations, gleams as a beacon of hope and peace amid chaos. This special time of year brings with it the reminder of the ultimate gift of love and salvation that was given to humanity.

The birth of Jesus Christ, celebrated on Christmas day, symbolizes a new beginning, a promise of redemption, and a source of comfort and joy for all who believe. It is a time to reflect on the blessings we have, to share kindness and compassion with others, and to rejoice in the spirit of unity and goodwill that permeates the air. Christmas is not just a holiday; it is a sacred time of renewal and rejuvenation, a time to connect with our faith, our loved ones, and the true meaning of life. Let us embrace the gift of Christmas with open hearts and grateful souls, spreading love and peace to all those around us.

Scripture:

Isaiah 9:6

For to us a child is born, to us a son is given, and the government will be on His shoulders. And He will be called Wonderful Counselor, Mighty God, Everlasting Father, Prince of Peace."

Devotional: The Big Pause

Christmas is a season for reflection on the invaluable gift of Jesus Christ, whose birth brought salvation and peace to our world. Isaiah 9:6 shows us His nature—Wonderful Counselor, Mighty God, Everlasting Father, Prince of Peace. His birth signifies more than just a moment in history.

God's ways are unexpected, as the nativity reminds us. The world's savior wasn't born in a palace; his birthplace was a humble stable. Shepherds, not kings, heard the news of his arrival. This humility and simplicity reveal God's freely given grace to all, regardless of social standing or life's events.

May the wonder of Christ's birth fill your heart this Christmas. Contemplate His peace and the hope He gives. Amid the holiday frenzy, remember Christmas is about the manger, the gift of Emmanuel, "God with us".

May the light of Christ shine through you this season. Spread His love, show compassion to the needy, and reflect His glory in your actions. Christmas is longer than just one day!

Prayer:

Heavenly Father, I thank You for Jesus Christ, the world's light and my soul's Savior. What an incredible gift. This Christmas, may I experience the awe of His birth and the happiness of His love. Guide me to be a beacon of His light, spreading peace and hope to those around me, reflecting the peace and hope that only He provides. May this season be a reminder of Your boundless grace and the promise of everlasting life. I give thanks for Emmanuel, God with us. Amen.

Reflective Questions:

1. How does the birth of Christ shape your understanding of God's love?

2. In what ways can you keep Christ at the center of your Christmas celebrations?

3. How can you share the joy of Christmas with someone who may struggle this season?

4. What does Emmanuel—"God with us"—mean to you personally?

**AUTHOR'S NOTE IN CLOSING:

Please remember me in your prayers. I am working daily to provide you with the best in Christian help. Please remember to order my other books from the following website or Amazon.com. Thank you.

Https://drcharlescravey.com

You may also contact me on that website for any responses. God bless you.

www.ingramcontent.com/pod-product-compliance
Lightning Source LLC
Chambersburg PA
CBHW030825090426
42737CB00009B/882